The Caucasian Republics

The Caucasian Republics

MARGARET KAETER

INTRODUCTION BY JUSTIN BURKE

®

Facts On File, Inc.

Nations in Transition: The Caucasian Republics

Text copyright © 2004 by Margaret Kaeter; Introduction by Justin Burke

Facts On File, Inc.
132 West 31st Street
New York NY 10001

Library of Congress Cataloging-in-Publication Data

Kaeter, Margaret.
  The Caucasian republics/Margaret Kaeter; introduction by Justin Burke.
    p. cm.—(Nations in transition)
  Includes bibliographical references and index.
  ISBN 0-8160-5268-9
  1. Transcaucasia—Juvenile literature. 2. Azerbaijan—Juvenile literature. 3. Georgia (Republic)—Juvenile literature. 4. Armenia (Republic)—Juvenile literature. [1. Transcaucasia. 2. Azerbaijan. 3. Georgia (Republic). 4. Armenia (Republic)] I. Title. II. Series.
  DK509.K25 2004
  947.5—dc22   2003025472

Text design by Erika K. Arroyo
Cover design by Nora Wertz
Maps by Sholto Ainslie © Facts On File

Printed in the United States of America

MP FOF 10 9 8 7 6 5 4 3 2 1

This book is printed on acid-free paper.

CONTENTS

CAUCASIAN REPUBLICS: PHYSICAL FEATURES

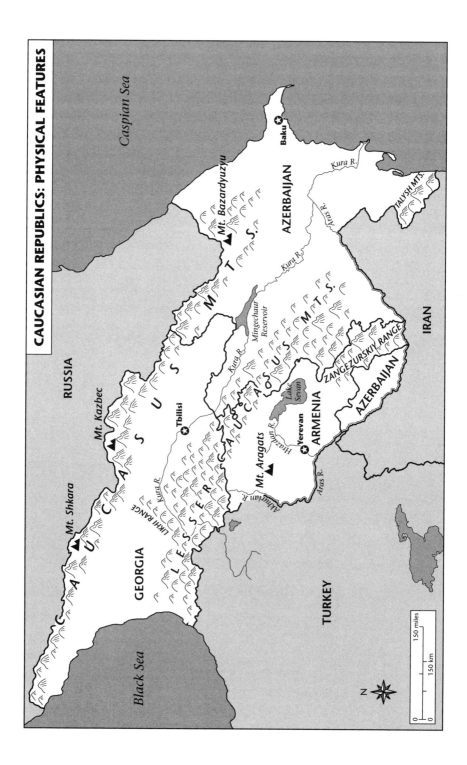

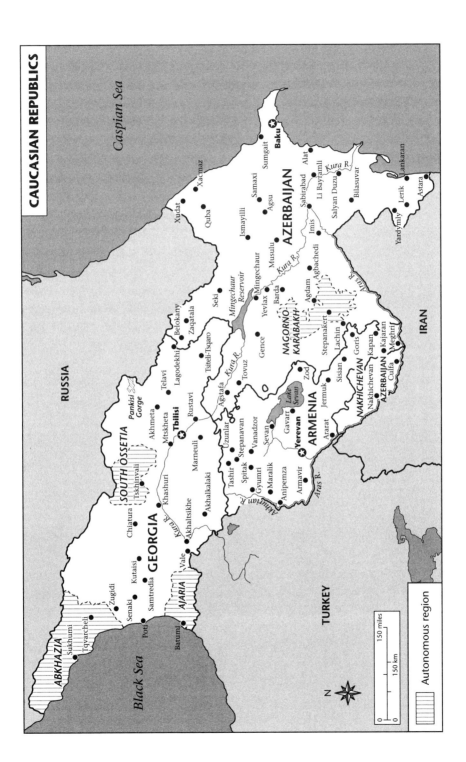

CAUCASIAN REPUBLICS

Caspian Sea

Black Sea

RUSSIA

TURKEY

IRAN

GEORGIA

ARMENIA

AZERBAIJAN

ABKHAZIA

AJARIA

SOUTH OSSETIA

NAGORNO-KARABAKH

NAKHICHEVAN

Baku

Tbilisi

Yerevan

Sumgait

Samaxi

Agsu

Xacmaz

Quba

Xudat

Ismayilli

Musulu

Yevlax

Barda

Gence

Agdam

Agbachedi

Stepanakert

Lachin

Goris

Sisian

Kapan

Kajaran

Meghri

Culfa

Nakhichevan

Jermuk

Ararat

Zod

Gavarr

Sevan

Vanadzor

Stepanavan

Spitak

Gyumri

Tashir

Maralik

Anipemza

Armavir

Uzunlar

Tovuz

Agstafa

Rustavi

Telavi

Lagodekhi

Tsiteli-Tsqaro

Belokany

Zaqatala

Seki

Mingechaur

Mingechaur Reservoir

Akhmeta

Mtskheta

Marneuli

Akhaltsikhe

Akhalkalaki

Khashuri

Vale

Chiatura

Kutaisi

Samtredia

Senaki

Zugidi

Tqvarcheli

Sukhumi

Poti

Batumi

Pankisi Gorge

Tskhinvali

Kura R.

Akhurian R.

Aras R.

Lake Sevan

Li Bayramli

Salyan Duzu

Alat

Sabirabad

Imis

Bilasuvar

Yardymly

Lerik

Astara

Lankaran

Kura R.

Aras R.

Autonomous region

N

150 miles

150 km

0

0

INTRODUCTION

For centuries, the Caucasus, the mountainous region wedged between the Black and Caspian Seas, existed in relative obscurity. However, political and economic developments in the 21st century are thrusting the Caucasus into the international spotlight.

Understanding the history and the culture of the three Caucasus states—Armenia, Azerbaijan, and Georgia—is increasingly important. Events in the region have a greater potential than ever to affect global developments.

The Caucasus sits on the fault line between two of the world's great religions—Christianity and Islam. Armenia and Georgia are both predominantly Christian nations, while the overwhelming majority of Azerbaijan's population is Muslim. For the past 15 years, the Caucasus has proved to be an especially volatile region, in large part because of cultural differences among the region's many national groups. Caucasus states are still searching for ways to settle long-lasting conflicts, including those in Nagorno-Karabakh and Abkhazia.

If the international community succeeds in promoting peace in the region, overall global stability could be significantly enhanced. The Caucasus, in effect, could prove to be a lab that can produce ways to ease existing tension between the Christian and Islamic worlds. Conversely, if the international community fails to address existing problems it could potentially result in a rise of Islamic radicalism.

Besides the issues of peace and stability, the Caucasus is important for economic reasons. Large deposits of oil and gas have been discovered in the region, especially around the Caspian Sea. Efforts to develop those resources could have profound ramifications for the international economy. In particular, it could reduce American dependence on the Middle East as a supplier of oil and gas.

For about seven decades, from the early 1920s to the early 1990s, the three Caucasus countries were part of the Soviet Union. During that time, Communist authorities repressed local cultures and crushed any attempt to demonstrate individual initiative. Since the collapse of the Soviet Union in 1991, all three Caucasus countries have struggled to overcome the Communist legacy.

In particular, the revival of long-repressed cultural yearnings was a major factor in starting the fighting between Armenia and Azerbaijan over Nagorno-Karabakh, as well as in provoking civil warfare in the Abkhaz region of Georgia. Also, the Communist legacy is partly responsible for the widespread corruption and crime that is frustrating economic development in all three Caucasus countries.

Older people are finding it difficult to change their ways. Younger people, especially students, are better able to adapt to the new, post-Soviet conditions. It may be that permanent solutions to the current problems in the Caucasus will require time, allowing those who are kids today in Armenia, Azerbaijan, and Georgia to grow up and assume positions of authority.

—Justin Burke

PART I
History

From Prehistory to the Byzantine Empire

The Caucasus. For most people in North America, the word means very little. People might know that it is a mountain chain on the southern border of Russia. They likely have heard of the countries of Armenia, Georgia, and Azerbaijan but know very little about them other than that they used to be part of the Soviet Union. They may even know that Azerbaijan has large oil reserves that people in the United States and Europe are helping harvest. It is possible they have heard about ethnic conflicts, especially between Armenia and Azerbaijan.

But beyond that, few of us know much about the Caucasus region. It should not be a surprise. While the countries that comprise the Caucasus are truly ancient, they have had little immediate impact on the lives of most current Americans or Western Europeans. However, as Justin Burke points out in his introduction to this book, events in the region have an increasing effect on global developments.

The Caucasus Mountains mark a geological fault line where the continents of Asia and Europe grind against each other, creating some of the highest and most treacherous mountain ranges in the world. Throughout history, that fault line also has marked both a cultural and political line. The mountains offered a natural barrier for people from Iran and Turkey trying to reach Europe through Russia.

Yet it was a barrier that traders and warriors alike, including Marco Polo and Chinggis (Genghis) Khan, wanted to explore because it offered a narrow land passage between the Caspian and Black Seas. As a result, the countries we now call Georgia, Armenia, and Azerbaijan really started their lives as primitive highways, hosting traders on their way between Europe and Asia.

Soon, people from all the different ethnic groups traveling through the areas realized that they could make a living catering to the caravans running through their lands, guiding them through mountain passes and, in the meantime, siphoning the latest goods from both Europe and Asia for their own people. The word *Caucasus* derives from an Arabic phrase meaning, "mountain of many languages," likely referring to the fact that the people who settled the area were from many different lands.

The conquering nations left their marks, to be sure. All three countries have cultural traditions that bear resemblances to Turkish, Persian, and Russian culture. Yet all three also developed unique cultures strong enough to carry them through centuries of occupation by foreign people.

Perhaps the most interesting fact is that these three countries, sitting virtually side by side for millennia, have not merged into one culture. They have developed cultural traditions and maintained ethnic roots that make each of them unique.

Ancient History

Humans have inhabited the Caucasus since before 200,000 B.C. Archaeologists have discovered prehuman remains thought to be 1.7 million years old, and all three countries maintain that they were settled by descendants of Noah after his ark came to rest on Mount Ararat, now in Turkey.

Secular historians agree that the area's roots lie in the beginning of organized humanity. The area we know as the Caucasus was the northern border of what historians studying ancient civilizations call the Fertile Crescent. The area extends roughly from the eastern edge of the Mediterranean Sea, arching up to the Black Sea, then curving under the Caspian Sea. It includes the area between the Black and Caspian Seas.

The Fertile Crescent marks the first large movement of people to other lands. "No doubt it is much of the story of the appearance of the earliest civilizations there. A turmoil of racial comings and goings for three or four thousands years both enriched and disrupted this area, where our history must begin. The Fertile Crescent was to be for most of historic times a great crucible of cultures, a zone not only of settlement but of transit, through which poured an ebb and flow of people and ideas. In the end this produced a fertile interchange of institutions, language and belief from which stems much of human thought and custom even today."

Whether one credits Noah and his ark for transporting the first non-natives to the area or believes a more mundane explanation—that populations were expanding so quickly they needed to move—the Caucasus Mountains were, for centuries, the northern border of an expanding Eurasian population.

The area became known as a hotbed of metalworking during the Copper and Bronze Ages, from 6000 to 1000 B.C. Civilization was thriving in the area between the Caspian and Black Seas, with various tribes known as the Hittites, Kanes, Hatti, and Wahsusana. The invention of writing took place in Mesopotamia and was quickly brought back by traders, making this also one of the first literate areas of the world.

As the area continued to grow, both explorers and traders found reason to traverse the land. As a result, the area of the Caucasus became a natural route on the Great Silk Road, which brought goods from the Far East to the Black Sea and points beyond. Traders most commonly took the routes from Persia (now Iran) to Yerevan (in Armenia today) and farther north through the mountain passes on the east side of Mt. Aragats to the town of Tbilisi in Georgia. One ancient trading path along the Hrazdan River was used 3,000 years ago; today part of it is a highway frequently filled with trucks hauling goods from the south to the north of Armenia.

Between 1200 and 1176 B.C., the Bronze Age kingdoms faced their last fight against a mysterious intruder known as the People of the Sea. The people, known as Ahhiyawa, traveled with their families and were seeking new lands to settle as they made their way through Greece, into Asia Minor (including the Caucasus region), and on to the Near East. Many stopped to settle in the Caucasus area and were greeted as both friends and conquerors, depending on the locality. In the eighth century

WHO ARE THE CAUCASIANS?

The people who settled in the region known as the Caucasus some 6,000 years ago had very pale skin. In the 1800s, several anthropologists thought that all people with pale white skin had originated in the area. As a result, the term Caucasian became accepted as the term for anyone with white skin. Since that time, however, the theory has been disproved. Although the United States continues to call white-skinned people Caucasians, Europe and the rest of the world simply call them white.

B.C., the Medes, the original inhabitants of Iran, made their way into present-day Azerbaijan.

The Persian Empire

Several hundred years passed before the area became important enough for another empire to try to conquer. The region became vitally important to Persia because it helped expand trade into the north by providing passage over land and over sea. It contained lush farmland that could be settled. It also had a long coast on the Caspian Sea that allowed Persia to develop a strong navy.

By 521 B.C. all but the far western edge of modern-day Caucasia had enough people and was an important enough trade route that it was conquered by Darius the Great and made a satellite of the Persian Empire. In fact, Azerbaijan's name is derived from the Persian word *azar*, meaning fire. This refers to the Zoroastrian temples that contain fires fueled by naturally occurring crude oil near the earth's surface. Zoroastrianism was the primary religion in the Persian Empire and the sacred fire symbolized the Zoroastrian god, Ahura Mazda. Many of these temples are still visible today and some even have burning fires.

By 500 B.C., the Persian Empire extended from the Balkans and North Africa in the west to India in the east. It was the largest and most powerful empire of the ancient world. The state of Armenia was a Persian satrapy (province) that included what today is northeastern Turkey, all of Armenia, and parts of Azerbaijan.

The Caucasus region played a key role in the Persian Empire's collapse. As soon as culture began to develop in western Europe, it began to migrate to the Black Sea coasts. The remains of Greek trading posts have been found from as early as the sixth century B.C.

Persia, under Cyrus II the Great (r. 559–530 B.C.), conquered the area on the coast, known as Ionia, as a way to gain a foothold on Europe but the residents proved very difficult. Around 500, the Ionian city of Miletus began a revolt that spread to all the Ionian cities. Miletus sought help from Greece and was granted some ships. However, the rebellion ultimately failed, and Ionia became a tribute-paying part of the Persian Empire. Until the Greeks liberated the area in 479 B.C.

The Greek king Alexander the Great (r. 336–323) was able to use this toehold as a launching pad to conquer the Persian Empire by 329 B.C. He defeated the Persians quickly and seized most of their empire for Macedonia. By the time of his death in 323 B.C. at the age of 33, he had conquered the entire known civilized world and created an enormous empire that spread from Greece to India.

After Alexander the Great died, his empire quickly fell apart. For the Caucasus, this meant a period of bouncing back and forth between rulers. The land and its boundaries changed hands many times, most often floating between Roman and Persian rule as the two states continually tried to steal land from each other.

Roman Control

By 190 B.C., Prince Artashes, the governor of Greater Armenia, a province of Syria, was able to pull together the nearby lands, including most of what today are the Caucasus republics and form an independent kingdom. He built the city of Artasha, and the country enjoyed peace and prosperity as Artashes and his successors looked to Greece for inspiration, as evidenced by several Greek inscriptions found in the royal residences of that time.

By the year 100 B.C., though, the Roman state began to take interest in the area. Tigranes I (d. 56 B.C.) of Greater Armenia struggled against the Roman Empire's push to rule the area and eventually extended the Armenian borders from the Caspian Sea to Egypt, gaining full control over the territories. He conquered provinces in Syria, Cappadocia (modern-day central Turkey), and Mesopotamia as well as Palestine. He united all the Armenian lands and built four large cities in different parts of his empire, all called Tigranakert.

In 69 B.C., Tigrane's expansion could no longer stand up to the Roman armies. They launched several offensives and, at the age of 75, Tigranes II was forced to sign a peace treaty that yielded several lands to Rome. Tigranes was able to keep some of the land, including present-day Armenia, and he remained an influential leader and adviser to the Roman conquerors. However, his son, Artavazd, an artistic and arrogant personality who preferred writing Greek plays and poems, squandered his inheritance and Armenia soon became a vassal state of the Roman Empire.

After the fall of the Western Roman Empire in 476, the land remained a pawn in the battle between the Byzantine Empire (the successor of the Eastern Roman Empire) and Persia for several centuries. At various times, the Byzantine Empire, based in Constantinopole (present-day Istanbul) appointed kings of small areas as conditions of treaties with Persia. Minor squabbles between local leaders also created ever-changing borders within the region.

THE SHROUD OF TURIN

According to legend, Tigranes I's nephew Abgar took control of Armenia after Artavazd died. He is said to have been a poor ruler who simply strengthened Rome's power over the land. However, after moving to Edessa, he heard about the miracles of Jesus Christ. Already old and ailing, Abgar wrote to Jesus and asked him to visit Edessa. Jesus did not accept the offer but wrote a response to Abgar's request. Legend says that after Christ's ascension, Thaddaeus, one of the disciples, arrived in Edessa bringing a piece of cloth that some researchers identify as the Shroud of Turin. Although recently discredited, for many centuries people believed the shroud contained the actual image of Christ's face.

While no single religion dominated the region at this time, in the year 301, Christianity became Armenia's official religion, making it the world's first Christian nation. Georgia soon followed, declaring Christianity its state religion in 330. Little changed in daily practice of religion or the daily lives of the people. The area was still a thoroughfare for traders and built its economy on that fact.

NOTE

p. 8 "'No doubt it is much of the story . . .'" Roberts, J. M. *History of the World* (Middlesex, England: Penguin Books, 1997), p. 45.

2
ARAB, TURKISH, AND MONGOL RULE

In the early seventh century, a merchant named Muhammad began preaching a new religion to fellow Arabs of the Arabian Peninsula. His belief that there is only one God, Allah, soon gained many followers. By the time of his death in 632, Muhammad had gained the adherence of many Arab tribes. After his death, his followers began a campaign of conquest, a holy war to spread their religion to the entire world.

Thus was the beginning of Islam and its spread into Asia Minor, including the Caucasus region. In 640, the Arabs first invaded the area and began to establish control. Over the next 120 years, the Muslim army continued to spread, stopping only when it reached France on the west and China on the East. The northern frontier was set along the Caucasus Mountains after a great Arab defeat at the hands of the Khazars in northern Azerbaijan.

Having been invaded on and off again since the beginning of recorded history, and possibly feeling resentment toward Byzantine religious orthodoxy, the rest of the Caucasus region put up little resistance to its new rulers. Some areas, such as the coastal region around the Caspian Sea, were nearly completely converted to Islam, while the more western areas continued to have a more blended culture.

More and more Arabs mixed with the local inhabitants and "the indigenous elites underwent an administrative and linguistic arabiza-

The Blue Mosque, here shown in the 1910s, is the only Persian mosque in Yerevan still preserved. Built in 1765, its portal and minaret were decorated with fine tile work. (Courtesy Library of Congress)

tion." By the mid-eighth century, when the more ruthless Abbasids controlled the Arab empire, Arabic was the language of government and business.

While under Arab power, the region reached a Golden Age. Armenia (which included modern-day Armenia as well as much of modern-day Georgia, Turkey, and Azerbaijan) built valuable trading relationships with other nations and saw a great deal of advancement in both trade and industry. Citizens enjoyed the freedom to build their own businesses catering to the many traders traversing their lands.

The arts also underwent significant advancement during this time, building on the skills developed through contacts with the Far East and western Europe. Potters advanced Chinese glazing and firing techniques. Carpet weavers created intricate designs based on Arabic symbolism. And, seeking to create even more beautiful places to worship their God than the Byzantine Empire had created, architects built on an elaborate scale.

This period also ushered in the first age of mass communication. Paper was being manufactured in the late 700s in the Arab city of Baghdad. The

Arabs took this invention and translated nearly every important written document from every culture under Arabic control. Many of these documents have since been lost in other languages and have yet to be translated from Arabic into a Western language.

Abbasid rule in the area ended in 946 when a Persian general deposed a caliph (Muslim leader) and inserted his own, creating the Bagratid dynasty. Under Queen Tamar, who ruled in the late 12th and early 13th centuries, the area reached another Golden Age. Music and literature were well-developed during this time, as well as the fine arts of sculpture and painting.

A clan of nomadic Turkmen tribes, called the Seljuks, were looking to create an empire, seizing Persia and then Iraq, and pushing into what is now southern Georgia and western Armenia in the 11th century. Although they never conquered the entire area of the Caucasus, the Turkish influence in the Caucasus would prove important in later years.

Mongol Rule

At the same time, a dynamic leader was beginning to create a following far to the east of the Caucasus. Having risen to the title of khan of his people by the 1190s, he quickly became leader of all Mongol tribes and was given the title Chinggis Khan. While his birthdate is uncertain, by the time he died in 1227, he had become the greatest conqueror in history.

In 1218, having defeated much of China and Manchuria, Chinggis Khan turned to the west in what he saw as a "divine mission" to rule the world. Although he was not as ruthless as often portrayed, he was infuriated when a Persian prince mistakenly killed his envoys. Chinggis Khan subsequently stormed through Persia, swung north through the Caucasus region into south Russia, and returned along the other side of the Caspian Sea. This was accomplished by 1223.

Chinggis Khan died in 1227, but his son Ogodai returned to the west in 1236, using the Caucasus region and the Caucasus Mountains as a gateway to Russia and the Black Sea. To achieve this, the Mongols reestablished security along the Great Silk Road, which enabled revived trade between Europe and Asia.

WHY WAS CHINGGIS KHAN SUCCESSFUL?

Many scholars have pondered how Chinggis (Genghis) Khan could lead an army to conquer nearly all of Europe and Asia. The reason is not that he was a great warrior but that he was a true leader, militarily, spiritually, and administratively. Among his qualities:

- He tolerated religious diversity. Those who submitted peacefully had little to fear.
- His soldiers were well-trained in the art of siege warfare.
- He only used warfare when negotiation failed.
- He moved only after doing reconnaissance and collecting intelligence regarding his foes.
- He recruited specialists from his captives. For example, he enlisted a Turkish captive to create a written Mongol language.
- He was organized. Chinese civil servants organized the conquered territories for revenue purposes.
- He set up communications areas along main roads to look after messengers and agents.
- He encouraged the rebuilding of roads and cities so he could quickly build trade between China and Europe.

While the administrative structure actually helped the region thrive through this period, the era of the khans had another impact on the region. The bulk of the Mongol army was made up of Turkish soldiers whose tribes had been absorbed by the Mongol advance across Eurasia. As these soldiers settled in the Caucasus region, the population slowly and subtly shifted from Persian roots to Turkish. Persian cities and cultural areas such as Zoroastrian temples were destroyed as the area was transformed to Turkish Islam.

Ottoman Empire

By the 15th century, the Mongols could no longer keep their large empire together. As the Caucasus region had been enjoying its revived status as a trade crossroads, Turkey was piecing together its past. Osman (1258–1326), a charismatic "warrior of the faith" became the founder of the Ottoman Empire, which soon stretched into the Balkans and part of Anatolia (modern-day Turkey). Following the death of Tamerlane, the last great Mongol conqueror in Asia Minor, in 1405, the Ottoman Turks invaded Asia Minor and by the beginning of the 16th century held all of it.

One notable exception was the eastern area of the Caucasus. Persia continued to try to reclaim its empire by mobilizing attacks in this area. The area was chronically disputed between the two countries for the next two centuries. Interestingly, the Safavids, the rulers of Persia at the time, had originally been Turks, but through years of conquest and intermarriage, they became a distinct group that wanted to overthrow the Ottomans.

As the Ottomans began to overtake the Byzantine Empire, the borders in the Caucasus region continued to shift back and forth between the Safavids and the Ottomans. In 1553, the Safavids held the eastern half of present-day Georgia and all of present-day Azerbaijan. The Ottomans held Azerbaijan from 1578 to 1603. In 1615, having gained control of the entire area, the Persian ruler, Shah Abbas I (r. 1588–1629), solidified his control by deporting thousands of people.

In the 1720s, the Ottomans attempted another conquest, but the Persians expelled them again. Persia then placed the Georgian kingdom of Kartli under the rule of royalty descended from the Bagratids, setting the stage to create most of modern-day Georgia. In 1747, Nadir Shah, the ruler of Persia, was assassinated in a palace coup. His kingdom quickly fragmented into many small regions, leaving the Caucasus region once again ripe for conquering.

NOTES

p. 11 "Having been invaded on and off again . . ." Roberts, J. M. *History of the World* (Middlesex, England: Penguin Books, 1997), p. 321.

p. 11 "More and more Arabs mixed with the local inhabitants . . ." Roberts, J. M. *History of the World*, p. 324.

p. 14 "Many scholars have pondered . . ." Roberts, J. M. *History of the World*, p. 367.

p. 14 "Osman (1258–1326), a charismatic 'warrior of the faith' . . ." Roberts, J. M. *History of the World*, p. 373.

3
CZARIST RUSSIA

As the 1700s came to a close, the world was changing dramatically. The Americas were being settled. Napoleon, rising out of the chaos of the French Revolution, began his conquest of Europe. Prussia was formed from the German Provinces of Brandenburg, Pomerania, Danzig, West Prussia, and East Prussia under the leadership of King Friedrich II (Friedrich the Great). The Russian Empire, occupying the vast area east of Europe and the northern side of the Caucasus was beginning to look for expansion opportunities in the Caucasus.

The Caucasus region was in such disarray that it is little surprise czarist Russia had a relatively easy time obtaining rule of the land. In Georgia, for example, local kings had had a difficult time uniting to fend off the Ottoman Turks and Persians. In 1783, Erekle II (c. 1720–1798), king of Kartli-Kakheti, turned to Russia for protection against Persian conquest. He accepted Russian vassalage in return for Russia's guarantee that his kingdom's borders would not change. However, Russia took a firmer hand in controlling the country. After his death, Russia annexed the eastern Georgian kingdom to the Russian Empire in 1801.

That scene played out again and again as Russia fought two Russo-Persian wars from 1804 to 1813 and from 1826 to 1828. In the end, Russia ended up with all the Persian territory north of the Aras River. It had become the first European power to extend its rule into the Middle East.

Russian expansion into Persian and Ottoman territory slowed in the 1850s as the leaders focused their attention on Europe. Between 1853 and 1856, the Russians were defeated in the Crimean War, which they fought against several European powers. They also continued to fight the Persians in addition to the Turks to gain greater control over the Caucasus. With an army split on two fronts, the conquest was difficult but, by 1860, they had completed their conquest of the Caucasus region between the Black and Caspian Seas.

Russia saw this area as a colony and was content to exploit it for its needs while allowing the local people to go about their daily lives without interference whenever possible.

Georgia

Georgia was perhaps the largest benefactor of the three countries in the Caucasus region. The area contained lush farmland and forests as well as

THE GEORGIAN MILITARY HIGHWAY

Long before the first people settled in Georgia, travelers and traders were making their way through the Caucasus Mountains, following rivers through valleys that lay between the steep mountains. The route was especially important to the kings of Iberia, a kingdom founded in the eastern part of present-day Georgia, between the sixth and fourth centuries, that was allied to the Romans. Their capital, Mtskheta, was at the southern end of the route. The journey was not easy; it took three days, and at times people had to walk single file. A chain of stone watchtowers was built along the route so an alarm could be passed when invaders were coming.

In 1803, Russian general Yermolov began to construct a bigger road on the same route. Today it is called the Georgian Military Highway. Although rail and air routes have supplanted its strategic importance, it was still used as an important military artery during both the first and second world wars.

A train maneuvers the Tkvebulski curves in turn-of-the-century Georgia. (Courtesy Library of Congress)

beautiful seashores. Czarist Russia exploited the area by creating a large timber industry and encouraging intensive farming practices.

Under Russian rule, the economy grew quickly. Russia provided education to most of the Georgian population, as well as raw materials to build factories and tractors to increase agricultural output. People enjoyed a good standard of living and had access to the basic necessities of life.

However, by 1900 nearly 60 percent of the land was owned by Russians, while most of the merchant class—the rising middle class that made its income from trading and selling goods—was Armenian. Some of the country's intellectuals formed a group known as "The Men of the '60s" and began to preach Georgian nationalism through their writings and speeches. The movement continued to grow into the early 1900s, eventually resulting in the deaths of 60 people when Russians broke up a Social Democrat meeting in Tbilisi on October 28, 1905.

Muslim religious leaders, called mullahs, pose outside their mosque in early 20th-century Batumi, Georgia. (Courtesy Library of Congress)

Armenia

Armenia was split nearly in half when Russia stopped conquering the region to turn its attentions toward Europe. The western half remained under Turkish control.

However, the part that was under Russian control looked as though it would prosper under czarist Russia. This new Armenia was inhabited by a large number of people with Russian roots and allegiances so Russia gave it a favored status. Industry was brought in and people were educated. In large part, Russia turned to Armenia as the leader and central figure of its lands south of the Caucasus Mountains.

This became a double-edged sword for both Russia and Armenia. On one hand, Russia was creating a more literate Armenia with loyalties to Russo-European culture. On the other hand, as Armenians became more literate, they started to conceive of themselves as separate from Russia. Add to this a concern among the Turks that Armenians were disregarding their Muslim roots. "The Armenians themselves changed dramatically in the mid-nineteenth century. An intellectual awakening influenced by Western and Russian ideas, a new interest in Armenian history, and an increase in social interaction created a sense of secular nationality among many Armenians. Instead of conceiving of themselves solely as a religious community, Armenians—especially the urban middle class—began to feel closer kinship with Christian Europe and greater alienation from the Muslim peoples among whom they lived."

Armenian leaders began to wonder if reform would come to the Russian Empire. As a result, in 1878, Armenian delegates appeared at the Congress of Berlin, where the European powers were negotiating the disposition of Ottoman territories after the defeat of the Ottoman Empire in the Russo-Turkish war. Armenian requests for European protection at this event were unrewarded, but the delegates did plant the seed for discussions about "the Armenian question" in later diplomatic events between Russia and Europe.

By the end of the 19th century, "the Armenians' tendency toward Europeanization antagonized Turkish officials and encouraged their view that Armenians were a foreign, subversive element in the sultan's realm." Armenians attempted a revolution between 1894 and 1897 to gain independence from Ottoman rule. In retaliation, the sultan ordered in 1895 the massacre of Armenians living in the empire, leading to an estimated 300,000 deaths by 1897.

Russians also were becoming suspect of Armenians. In 1903, Armenian churches and schools were closed and church property was confiscated. Armenians were massacred in several towns and cities in 1905, and 52 Armenian nationalist leaders in Russia were tried en masse for underground activities in 1912.

The Armenian population that remained in the Ottoman Empire after the 1895–97 massacres supported the 1908 revolution of the Committee of Union and Progress, better known as the Young Turks, who promised liberal treatment of ethnic minorities. However, after its revolution succeeded, the Young Turk government plotted elimination of the Armenians, who were a significant obstacle to the regime's evolving nationalist agenda.

Accusing the Armenians of aiding the Russian invaders during World War I (1914–1918), the Ottoman government ordered large-scale roundups, deportations, and killing of Armenians beginning in the spring of 1915. Estimates vary from 600,000 to 2 million deaths out of the prewar population of about 3 million Armenians. By 1917, fewer than 200,000 Armenians remained in Turkey. Although Armenians claim this was an act of attempted genocide, the Turks blame the deaths on famine and problems related to World War I.

Whatever the reason, this loss of population shifted the center of the Armenian population from the heartland of historical Armenia to the relatively safer eastern regions held by the Russians. Tens of thousands of refugees fled to the Caucasus with the retreating Russian armies after World War I, and the cities of Baku and Tbilisi filled with Armenians from Turkey. Between 1915 and 1917, Russia occupied virtually the entire Armenian part of the Ottoman Empire.

Azerbaijan Suffers

Azerbaijan fared badly under colonization. When oil was discovered in the Azerbaijani part of the Caspian Sea, the Russians quickly took advantage of this precious resource. In the late 1800s, Baku, the city on the large peninsula jutting into the Caspian Sea, became the fastest-growing city in the Russian Empire. The town experienced rapid industrialization and the rise of entrepreneurial, working, and intelligentsia classes. By 1900, Azerbaijan supplied most of Russia's oil.

With this industrialization came new concerns. Because the Russians did not plan to develop the country, industrialization was limited to one region and was centered on extracting oil rather than manufacturing anything. Many local Azerbaijanis lacked managerial qualifications, so czarist officials brought in Russians and Armenians to supervise development and to work as skilled labor.

The influx of Russians and Armenians into Baku created a segregated society; the Azerbaijanis remained poor and uneducated while the numerous newcomers received the highest-paying jobs in the oil industry. As a result, Russians and Armenians gained control of local government.

This was the beginning of a long tradition of tension between Azerbaijan and Armenia. The Russian Revolution of 1905, while unsuccessful in overthrowing czarist Russia, brought about a political awakening in Azerbaijan. People realized they did not have to be under the control of the wealthy Armenians who talked about the "Greater Armenia" being built from Armenia and Azerbaijan. The Azerbaijanis also resented the fact that the Armenians were being given more favors from czarist Russia. As a result, the interethnic tension following the 1905 upheaval in Russia resulted in massacres of large numbers of Armenians and Azerbaijanis.

The outbreak of World War I in 1914 brought hardships to every part of the Russian Empire. Although most of the Caucasus population were

The small village of Saatly, Mugan Steppe, is typical of small towns in turn-of-the-century Azerbaijan. (Courtesy Library of Congress)

These members of the 1919 Armenia republic cabinet had to deal with both Turkish and Russian invasions before they finally lost their jobs to become part of the Soviet Union. (Courtesy Library of Congress)

not involved directly in the war, high taxes and food shortages and other hardships imposed by the war set the stage for revolution.

NOTES

p. 19 "However by 1900 nearly 60 percent of the land was owned by Russians . . ." Buford, Tim. *Georgia with Armenia* (Guilford, Conn.: Globe Pequot Press, 2002), p. 19.

p. 21 "'The Armenians themselves change dramatically . . .'" U.S. Library of Congress. Armenia – National Self Awareness. www.countrystudies.us/armenia/8.htm. Downloaded February 17, 2004.

p. 21 "'The Armenians' tendency toward Europeanization . . .'" U.S. Library of Congress. Armenia – National Self Awareness. www.countrystudies.us/armenia/8.htm. Downloaded February 17, 2004.

4

THE CAUCASIAN REPUBLICS UNDER SOVIET RULE

In March 1917, the Russian Revolution overthrew the czar and put an end to the Russian Empire. All three Caucasian countries experienced a period of independence.

They briefly aligned in the Federative Republic of Transcaucasia, in an attempt to provide more power to negotiate treaties and trade relations. However, the union soon fell apart. Armenia subsequently fought wars against its neighboring republics in an attempt to control territories predominantly inhabited by Armenians, such as the region of Nagorno-Karabakh held by Azerbaijan.

The brief period of independence came to an end in 1920/21. From the spring of 1920 through 1921, the Red Army was sent into the Caucasus region to begin a campaign to control the three Caucasus countries. It met almost no resistance in Azerbaijan, since most of the Azerbaijani army was busy with an Armenian uprising in Uarabakh. As a result, in April 1920, Azerbaijan was the first to fall to Russia. Armenia fell to Russia by the end of the year, and Georgia fell in 1921.

All the countries suffered after Stalin obtained full rule of the Soviet Union in the late 1920s. He directed the exportation or deportation to labor camps of many people even marginally suspected of opposing the Soviet regime. The Soviets also banned literature from popular authors, controlled the works of artists and musicians, and persecuted religious leaders, except for those of the Georgian Orthodox Church (see chapter 7).

The Transcaucasian Soviet Federated Socialist Republic

Joseph Stalin, a Georgia native, was in charge of nationality affairs after the Russian Revolution of 1917. He decided to merge Armenia with Georgia and Azerbaijan. This union was to form a new political entity called the Transcaucasian Soviet Federated Socialist Republic (SFSR). The United Soviet Socialist Republics (USSR) was founded in December 1922 with four constituent republics, one of which was

AUTONOMOUS REPUBLICS

The former Soviet republics are one of the few places in the world containing political boundaries within boundaries. Other countries will have distinct ethnic minorities living in large regions. The groups may develop some local laws and certainly adhere to local customs (much as individual U.S. states have their own laws), but they are not separated from the rest of the country; they obey the laws of the nation first.

How did this happen? In the early days of the Soviet Union, Stalin was charged with drawing the borders for the union's republics. He, in agreement with all the Communist commisars, reasoned that the outlying republics, especially, would be easier to control by Moscow if their populations were split apart. In this way, they could not physically group together to plan subversive actions. It was, in a classic military sense, a tactic of "divide and conquer."

After just a few years as autonomous republics, Moscow changed their titles to autonomous regions and gave them less control over their own local governance. With the fall of the Soviet Union, many of the regions have re-adopted the term "republic" as a way to show the Transcaucasian SFSR However, in 1936, the Transcaucasian republic was dissolved, and the countries became constituent Soviet republics.

ARMENIA

Under the Soviet system, many industries were set up in Armenia to manufacture goods for other Soviet republics. Likewise, the precious metals mined in Armenia were used in other Soviet republics. Unfortunately, this buildup in production gave few benefits to the Armenians and resulted in the pollution of their land and rivers.

The Soviet government also encouraged development of agriculture in Armenia, however, with disastrous long-term effects. To make much of the land usable, the managers of the state-owned farms had to use large amounts of fertilizers and pesticides that eventually leached into the drinking water.

the countries in which they are imbedded that they wish to govern themselves.

In Azerbaijan, for example, Nagorno-Karabakh was made an autonomous republic, even though it contained mostly ethnic Armenians. The Armenians have never liked the situation and, with the demise of the Soviet Union, have worked hard to be reunited with Armenia.

Likewise, Stalin created Naxcivan, the separated region of Azerbaijan located on the western border of Armenia. While not quite as tense a situation as Nagorno-Karabakh, Azerbaijan continues to view Naxcivan culturally as part of its country. Georgia also was sliced into different pieces during the 1920s as Stalin continued to direct nationality affairs. For example, in July 1921 the Ajarian Autonomous Soviet Socialist Republic was formed within Georgia. Abkhazia was initially a separate Soviet republic, but in 1921 it was merged with Georgia, and in 1930 it was downgraded to the status of an autonomous republic. In April 1922, the Soviet government created the political entity of South Ossetia and designated it an autonomous region within Georgia, while its northern counterpart on the other side of the Greater Caucasus, North Ossetia (now Alania), became part of Russia.

In 1985, when Mikhail Gorbachev became leader of the USSR, Armenians began to have a say in their life again. Gorbachev introduced *glasnost* (meaning "openness"), a program that allowed open discussion of controversial issues. Armenians initially demonstrated against the environmental problems in their republic. They met with some success when minor resolutions dealt with key areas of the environment, such as the rivers.

BLACK JANUARY

In February 1988, the autonomous region of Nagorno-Karabakh created a spark that renewed ethnic conflict between Armenia and Azerbaijan. More than 1 million Armenians rallied for annexation of the area at that time, but Gorbachev refused to allow its transfer to Armenia. The result was a violent anti-Armenian backlash in Azerbaijan, peaking with a massacre of Armenians in Sumgait. In response, Armenians began to deport Azerbaijanis living in Armenia and Karabakh. A similar attack on Azerbaijanis occurred in the Armenian town of Spitak. Large numbers of refugees left Armenia and Azerbaijan as pogroms began against the minority populations of the respective countries.

Following even more tensions, in 1989, Gorbachev proposed enhanced autonomy for Nagorno-Karabakh. However, this satisfied neither Armenians nor Azerbaijanis, and a long and inconclusive conflict erupted. In September 1989, Azerbaijan began an economic blockage of Armenia's vital fuel and supply lines through its territory, which had carried about 90 percent of Armenia's imports from the other Soviet republics.

Violent riots targeting ethnic Armenians erupted in Baku in January 1990. Moscow decided to intervene, sending Soviet tanks into the Azerbaijani capital. Armenian inhabitants were evacuated, but more than 130 people were killed and more than 1,000 were injured. Merchant ships blockading the harbor were shelled or sunk.

The Soviet government also banned public demonstrations and outlawed radical nationalist organizations. The result was a return to disarray. Many of the dissident leaders were arrested and the remaining members seemed split between conservative and more liberal factions. In elections held in September 1990, although other parties were rep-

In the meantime, another hardship had hit Armenia in 1988. An earthquake centered near Spitak in the northern part of the country left more than 35,000 people dead and more than 400,000 people homeless.

As the small country of Armenia neared the end of Soviet rule and once again looked inward for its governance, it faced many problems: hostile neighbors and hostility toward its neighbors, polluted land, and an industrial system unsuited for its role as an independent country.

resented on the ballot, the Communists won nearly 90 percent of the votes in some important contests.

The people quickly began referring to the January events as "Black January," and they accused the Communists of rigging the September elections. Tensions between Armenia and Azerbaijan continued, often erupting into fighting that took many lives. In the end, these events strengthened popular support for independence.

Relations between Armenia and Azerbaijan have always been tense. This 106-year-old Armenian woman still felt the threat as she guarded her home near the Azerbaijani border in 1990. (UN/DPI Photo by Armineh Johannes)

AZERBAIJAN

At first it looked as though Azerbaijan might be better off for being part of the Soviet Union. The government of Azerbaijan was allowed to put its own people into top positions. The USSR also brought more industry to the country and educated everyone.

By the late 1920s, however, it became clear that everything was not good. As with all the Soviet republics, Azerbaijani nationalists and intellectuals were killed or deported. The Soviet regime forced farmers to collectivize, combining private lands into large, state-operated farms. Farmers protested but were beaten, deported, and killed for their opposition. By 1940, Azerbaijan had lost more than 120,000 people in this Great Purge.

The change in the Azerbaijani alphabet was among the more damaging aspects of Soviet rule for Azerbaijan. By changing it from traditional Arabic script to the Russian Cyrillic letters, it effectively cut Azerbaijani people off from traditional Islamic culture.

Although World War II had little effect on the country, life did not remain easy as Azerbaijan entered the second half of the 20th century. The country's crucial oil industry lost its high value to the Soviet Union with the discovery of oil in Siberia. This, in turn, meant that Moscow would invest less in industry in Azerbaijan. By the 1960s, Azerbaijan had the lowest rate of growth in productivity and economic output among the Soviet republics.

The Azerbaijani population remained relatively content throughout the next two decades, though. Unlike their sister republics, Armenia and Georgia, they did not have a dissident movement throughout this period. Both the farm and the city dwellers were making progress toward a better standard of living.

GEORGIA

Although he was a native Georgian, Stalin apparently felt little love for his country. As in all Soviet republics, he ordered massive arrests and executions of party officials, intellectuals, and rank-and-file citizens during the purges of the late 1930s. During World War II (1939–45) Stalin ordered the deportation of entire minority groups from the Soviet Union, although he spared religious leaders of the Georgian Orthodox Church.

JOSEPH STALIN

Georgia's most famous—and infamous—son is Joseph Stalin. Born Josef Vissarionovich Djugashvili on December 21, 1879, in the small town of Gori, he rose to become the leader of the Soviet Union and headed one of the most ruthless killing campaigns in the 20th century. He and his compatriots sought to rid the Soviet Union of any intellectual, anti-communist, and religious opposition. As a result, more than 45 million people were killed.

Young Joseph did not appear headed for infamy, though. His mother cleaned laundry and his father was an alcoholic cobbler. He was born with a webbed left foot and had a crooked left arm after he was run over by a cart. He did so well at a church school that he was sent to seminary. However, he was expelled for revolutionary politics and became an accountant at the Tbilisi Meteorological and Geophysical Observatory.

He participated in a violent May Day demonstration in 1901 and then was arrested in 1902 after helping organize strikes in the Rothschild oil plants in Batumi. He was sent to Siberia but escaped in 1904. In 1903, the Social Democrats split into two groups, and Stalin, a name he adopted because it suggest "man of Steel" in Russian, supported the radical Bolsheviks and their leader, Vladimir Lenin. Between 1902 and 1913, he was frequently arrested but always escaped.

In 1912, Lenin appointed Stalin to the Bolshevik Central Committee, although he was arrested again and lived in a Siberian gulag until the March revolution of 1917. In 1922, he became general-secretary of the party's Central Committee, and when Lenin died in 1924, Stalin maneuvered himself into the Soviet Union's leadership position. He began as a moderate, advocating an end to revolution, but his actions became more and more dictatorial and cruel as the years went on.

Stalin died on March 5, 1953. Both Nikita Khrushchev, his successor, and Mikhail Gorbachev, the last leader of the Soviet Union, denounced Stalin's crimes. In Georgia, many continue to see him as a strong leader who had to make difficult decisions; his crimes often are regarded as the price of reform.

Abkhazia brought many problems for Georgia during Soviet rule. Under Georgia's 1921 constitution, this northwestern region was autonomous. Stalin made it an autonomous republic in 1930, but he also encouraged Georgians to move to the area so that, by 1989, almost half the population was Georgian. In 1989, students demanded that teaching at the University of Sukhumi be in Georgian rather than Abkhazian. The demonstration led to 14 deaths.

Little changed for Georgia from the time of Stalin's death until the 1980s. It remained a prime supplier of foodstuffs to other Soviet republics and a prime vacation spot for senior party members.

However, friction between the Georgian government and ethnic minorities increased after the Georgian Supreme Soviet passed a law establishing the Georgian language as the official state language in 1989. On April 9 of that year, demonstrators in Tbilisi demanded that Abkhazia remain a part of Georgia and that Georgia declare independence from the USSR. Soviet security forces attacked them, killing 19 and injuring many others. This further solidified anti-Soviet sentiment among Georgians.

Following Gorbachev's policies of glasnost and perestroika, many nations in Eastern Europe began holding elections that included candidates from political parties other than the Communist Party. November 1990 was the first time other political parties were allowed to participate in elections in Georgia since Soviet rule. The Communist Party of Georgia lost its monopoly, with the majority of votes going to the Round Table-Free Georgia coalition of pro-independence parties. Zviad Gamsakhurdia, the leader of the coalition and a longtime nationalist dissident, became chairperson of the new legislature and Georgia's de facto head of state.

NOTES

p. 28 "In February 1988, the autonomous region of Nagorno-Karabakh . . ." Federation of American Scientists: Military Analysis Network. www.fas.org/man/dod-101/ops/nar/nagorno-karabakh.htm. Downloaded May 2, 2003.

p. 30 "By the late 1920s, however, it became clear that everything was not good." Virtual Azerbaijan. http://scf.usc.edu~baguirov/azeri/azerbaijan4.htm. Downloaded March 3, 2003.

p. 31 "As a result, more than 45 million people . . ." Buford, Tim. *Georgia with Armenia* (Guilford, Conn.: Globe Pequot Press, 2002), p. 22.

PART II
The Caucasian Republics Today

5

ARMENIA

The Land and Its People

Nestled high in the Caucasus mountain plains that separate Russia from the Middle East, Armenia is one of the most secluded countries in the world. Its neighbors—Turkey to the west and southwest, Iran to the southeast, Azerbaijan to the south and east, and Georgia to the north—all have access to large seas. Armenia, however, sits landlocked, squashed in the middle of these larger countries. There is no way to enter or to leave the country except by traversing high mountain passes or by airplane.

Armenia, more than Georgia or Azerbaijan, lives and breathes the Caucasus Mountains. The small country contains some of the highest peaks in the Lesser Caucasus chain. Mount Aragats rests in the western part of the country and serves as one focal point for the country's agriculture, industry, and tourism. Mount Ararat, the 16,000-foot mountain that historically symbolizes the country for both foreigners and Armenians, lies slightly farther south in what is now Turkey.

With 11,500 square miles of land, Armenia is just slightly larger than the state of Maryland. However, much of that land is impossible to live on. About half of Armenia's land is more than one mile above sea level, and only 3 percent of the country lies below 2,000 feet. In most of Armenia, the land receives fewer than 10 inches of rain a year. It is very common for much of the country to experience severe drought at any time of year.

If it were not for the Caspian Sea, which lies several hundred miles to the east of Armenia, and the Black Sea, which lies several hundred miles

Although officially residing in Turkey today, Armenians are spiritually linked to Mount Ararat. It is said that Noah's ark rests on the mountain and Noah's great-great grandson was the first to settle in Armenia. (Courtesy Free Library of Philadelphia)

to the west of Armenia, the country would have extremely cold weather. However, those two large bodies of water bring more warm weather than is usually found at such high altitudes.

For example, summer temperatures are very similar to those in Arizona and New Mexico, with warm evenings and daytime highs reaching 100 degrees Fahrenheit. Spring and fall usually have temperatures more like those in the midwestern United States, ranging from 40 to 80 degrees with cooler evenings. Winter, because of the surrounding highlands, frequently brings temperatures like that in the northeastern United States, with highs rarely reaching 50 degrees Fahrenheit.

No matter what the temperature, because the country is high in the mountain plains and receives very little rain or snow, most of the days are sunny and bright. The few rain showers that occur in the spring rarely last more than an hour or two, and snowfalls are rarely more than a couple of inches, except on the mountain peaks.

Because of its unique geography, the country is divided into four regions. The northeastern area has folded back mountains. This area is one of the few natural sources of wealth for the country. The frequent earthquakes of several thousands years ago revealed large deposits of precious metals such as gold, copper, and zinc. The area also has some forest and small pockets of land suitable for raising livestock.

The central part of the country has many mountains that used to be volcanoes, with high plateaus lying between. The mountains are too high to serve as good land for farming, while the plateaus are made of dense volcanic rock. As a result, any water the area does receive from rain or mountain runoff does not sink into the soil but simply flows farther south. However, this durable rock makes an excellent building material used in most of the buildings in the country.

The southern part of Armenia is a broken network of valleys and deep gorges that show some good deposits of minerals and precious gems. More important, though, is the fact that in between these large cracks in the ground lies good farmland that produces some major crops of citrus fruits and vegetables. The grapes grown in this area are highly prized for making wine, and the area was so fertile that, during Soviet rule, it was able to provide enough fruits and vegetables for its own citizens while still having enough to send to nearby Georgia and Russia.

The northwest is a fairly flat plain, but it sits on very brittle fault lines in the earth's crust. These faults frequently shift, creating large-scale, severe earthquakes. The area has some deposits of minerals and some forested land that provides income for the residents. Some farmers are able to make a small living by raising potatoes, sheep, and beef cattle on the dry, hard land.

Because the country has so many different types of land, it has animal and plant habitats ranging from deserts to forests, marshland, and alpine meadows. As a result, Armenia has a larger variety of wildlife and plants than its neighbors. It has more than 3,500 species of plants and hundreds of different mammals, such as bear, deer, and squirrels. It also has nearly 350 types of birds because many migratory birds travel through Armenia to winter on the Caspian Sea.

The most striking—and most economically important—geographic feature in Armenia is Lake Sevan, one of the largest freshwater lakes in the world. Sitting in the north central area of the country, it takes up 5 percent of the country's entire land, or more than 600 square miles. It serves as an important source of water, as the Hrazdan River leaves it from the northwestern coast and flows through the country's capital city, Yerevan. Just south of Yerevan, the Hrazdan connects with the Aras River, which flows west to east along the southern border of the country. These two rivers help irrigate farmland and move products between the north and south of the country, while the lake itself serves as an important recreation spot for the country's citizens.

THE PEOPLE

Perhaps because the land is so difficult to live on, very few people move to Armenia. Unlike its neighbors, Georgia and Azerbaijan, Armenia never saw much immigration from people in other Soviet republics. As a result, the people are almost exclusively native Armenians.

The country has 3.8 million people, about the same as the state of Iowa. Ninety-three percent are ethnic Armenians. The remaining 7 percent of the population are Russians and Kurds.

While Armenians are not a diverse people, there are small pockets of people living in the mountains that do not share the typical Armenian

DID LAKE SEVAN CREATE ARMENIA?

Although Lake Sevan is not large, especially compared with the Great Lakes of North America, Armenia may not have existed at all if it were not for this body of water. Before the days of jet airplanes, Armenia was an important trade route from Iran and Turkey to Russia. Because Lake Sevan offered a convenient resting spot for nomadic people and traders, it became a place where people traded goods. Towns eventually built up around the lake, and people began to settle in the area. Had the lake not existed, it is likely no one would have stopped in this little patch of land while heading north. The result is that Armenia's geographic boundaries would have been completely swallowed by its neighbors, and its unique culture would not have developed.

An interesting note is that during the country's Silver Age, in the 1300s, the Italian explorer and trader Marco Polo (1234–1324) visited Armenia; it is likely he stayed at an inn on the south shore of Lake Sevan, the remains of which are still visible today.

Lake Sevan is a favorite spot for archaeologists because the Soviet Union lowered the lake to create hydroelectric power plants. This left centuries-old artifacts right in the open. Some of the roads around the lake travel the same routes taken by explorers and traders such as Marco Polo.

heritage. For example, about 60,000 Yezdi live in the highlands surrounding the Aragats and Hoktemberian peaks. This Kurdish sect remains isolated and practices Yezidism, a faith heavily influenced by Islam but also devoted to the ancient religions of Mithraism and Zoroastrianism.

With farming only a small industry in Armenia, and most of the country's mines being located within a few miles of a small town, it is not surprising that most of the native Armenians live in urban centers. More than two-thirds of the population live in cities and towns, while just 1.2 million people live on about 8,000 square miles of countryside. Most of these people are farmers in the valleys surrounding Mount Aragats.

The isolation this country and its people endure also has created a unique language. Armenian is an Indo-European language, but has no links with any other surviving language. It has borrowed some words from Persian and Turkish during the last two centuries but is most likely a combination of the many different trade languages spoken by the people traveling through the country in previous centuries. Because the country is so separated from its neighbors, the language was able to evolve and survive.

Armenia is a former republic of the Union of Soviet Socialist Republics. Although most people today speak Armenian at home and in the workplace, Russian remains an important language as Armenians seek to maintain a place in the broader world.

Most Armenians also are well educated. Because of the Soviet government's emphasis on free education, nearly all adults can read and write. Primary and secondary school are still free of charge and mandatory, even for people who live in rural areas. Many also go on to college or trade school. Because the country has good supplies of precious metals, the colleges produce many engineers. Likewise, because it has a tradition as a central trade route between the Middle East and Russia, the country also produces people well versed in international business.

Perhaps because the country's geography presents so many challenges, Armenians have the reputation as quick-thinking, purposeful people. Their roots lie with nomadic traders who set their sights on goals and worked to achieve them rather than assuming something was impossible. As a result, Armenians view themselves as self-reliant, even though the country's poor economic conditions continue to make them largely dependent on Russia.

THE NAGORNO-KARABAKH CONFLICT

In a December 1991 referendum boycotted by local Azerbaijanis, Armenians in Nagorno-Karabakh approved the creation of an independent state and quickly named their long-time leader, Robert Kocharian, as its president. A Supreme Soviet (legislature) was elected, and Nagorno-Karabakh appealed for world recognition. (No country recognizes the legitimacy of this new government except Armenia.)

As a strong supporter of Armenia and its efforts to obtain Nagorno-Karabakh, Kocharian began to rise in prominence. He became famous while he worked to solicit funds from Armenians living in other countries to rebuild the road that leads from Armenia to Nagorno-Karabakh's capital, Stepanakert. He felt this Lachin Corridor would be a major start in bringing the enclave back under Armenia's rule.

Soon after Kocharian came into power, Armenian separatists declared control of the region and parts of Azerbaijan, displacing almost 1 million Azerbaijanis but providing the means to open the Lachin Corridor. The result was a bloody war. By June 1992, ethnic Armenians had expelled all ethnic Azerbaijanis from the Nagorno-Karabakh region.

No resolutions to the conflict emerged during 1992, despite a number of attempted cease-fires. At the same time the attacks were launched on the Azerbaijani land surrounding Nagorno-Karabakh, an attack also was launched on the Azerbaijani enclave of Nakhichevan, the small, separated region of Azerbaijan located on the western border of Armenia. While troops of the former Soviet army remained stationed along the border with Turkey and Iran, an increasing number of clashes between Armenian and Azerbaijani militias were erupting in the northern portion of the region.

Subsequently, Azerbaijan mounted a counterattack in Nagorno-Karabakh and by early July had recaptured most of its northern sector. However, the land returned to Armenian control in the next few months.

In 1993, Armenian forces defeated the Azerbaijani army in several confrontations in Nagorno-Karabakh, which led to Armenian control of the region and of adjacent areas. Armenia enforced a blockade of Nakhichevan. In return, Azerbaijan prohibited any goods to enter Armenia from Azerbaijan. It also enlisted Turkey as an ally in the blockade. Since Armenia received most of its petroleum from Azerbaijan and

Turkey, the blockade was the first real advantage for Azerbaijan in the war for the Nagorno-Karabakh region.

Initial cease-fire agreements failed to hold until a May 1994 agreement was reached by Russia and the Organization on Security and Cooperation in Europe (OSCE), but negotiations to resolve the conflict continued unsuccessfully and sporadic fighting and shelling continued. More than 1.2 million Azerbaijanis have left the region for Azerbaijan.

In May 1995, Armenia withdrew from negotiations, charging Azerbaijan involvement in a Georgian Azerbaijani bombing that severed a pipeline carrying vital gas supplies to Armenia from Turkmenistan.

In May 1997, Turkey and Azerbaijan issued a joint declaration condemning Armenian aggression in Nagorno-Karabakh and asking Armenia to withdraw its troops from the region.

In September 1997, the OSCE proposed a "phased approach" as a political solution. Azerbaijan accepted the idea while Armenia endorsed it as a basis for further talks. Nagorno-Karabakh, however, did not accept it and demanded that all issues be resolved simultaneously.

For the next four years, the negotiations remained at a standstill. Azerbaijani, Nagorno-Karabakh and Armenian leaders have worked with international groups, but neither side was willing to change its position. In April 2002, Azerbaijani president Aliyev hinted that Azerbaijan might consider resuming military action if Armenia refused to make negotiating concessions.

Armenian forces and forces of the "Republic of Nagorno-Karabakh" continue to occupy 20 percent of Azerbaijan's territory. Exchanges of fire occur frequently along the border, causing both military and civilian casualties.

A military jeep drives along the Lachin corridor, which leads to Armenia from the enclave of Nagorno-Karabakh inside Azerbaijan. (AP Photo/Oleg Nikishin)

Government

Armenian citizens voted for independence from the former USSR on September 21, 1991, and Levon Ter-Petrossian, formerly a scholar and dissident, was elected Armenia's first president in October 1991. Ter-Petrossian immediately began to implement plans that would help build the economy and bring formerly Soviet-owned businesses back into private ownership.

On February 2, 1993, Ter-Pertrossian dismissed Prime Minister Khosrov Haroutiunian for having criticized government economic policies. Hrand Bagratian was named prime minister, but opposition parties quickly pressed for new elections, mounting large antigovernment demonstrations at the capital, Yerevan, throughout 1993 and 1994.

A new constitution adopted by a nationwide referendum in 1995 established a unitary multiparty republic. People are elected to a unicameral (one chamber) national assembly in two ways. Fifty-six people are elected from national party lists on a proportional basis based on the political parties citizens have selected. Seventy-five are elected from single-member districts by the citizens. The president has a great deal of power in this system, as he appoints the prime minister and various other government ministers who, in turn, appoint ministers for the country's various districts.

Ter-Petrossian was re-elected for another five-year term in September 1996. However, a large group of citizens (and international observers) claimed the election was a fraud. Three days of public demonstrations to protest the extremely slow vote count were held outside the national parliament in Yerevan. Ter-Petrossian's special police and soldiers brutally mowed down the protestors, and several people were killed.

On November 4, 1996, the president appointed Armen Sarkisian, former ambassador to the United Kingdom, to succeed Bagratian as prime minister. Bagratian resigned his post officially for personal reasons, but political insiders say, perhaps he was disconcerted by "the influence of growing popular discontent over the effects of the government's economic reforms." Although it appeared as though the gross domestic product was growing, wages were lower than ever and unemployment was rising. Sarkisian resigned on March 6, 1997, and was replaced by

Robert Kocharian, the president of the self-proclaimed Republic of Nagorno-Karabakh.

The appointment of Kocharian as prime minister seriously increased the tension between Armenia and Azerbaijan. Some, perhaps including Ter-Petrossian, felt it might provide renewed energy to negotiations regarding Nagorno-Karabakh, but Azerbaijan quickly accused Ter-Petrossian of provocation in the matter. By mid-April, fighting between Armenian and Azerbaijani forces broke out in two locations along the border. A peace plan drafted by the OSCE proposed giving the region autonomous status within Azerbaijan, but the plan also called for the withdrawal of the Armenian forces from Azerbaijan. Meanwhile, Kocharian announced that his government did not rule out the possibility of annexing Nagorno-Karabakh.

In September 1991, Ter-Petrossian suggested that he was willing to consider an arrangement in which an autonomous Nagorno-Karabakh would remain a part of Azerbaijan, putting him at odds with Prime Minister Kocharian. He was willing to compromise, he said, because he believed Armenia's economic potential was being "held hostage" to the conflict.

In what historians describe as a "velvet coup d'état," Ter-Petrossian resigned in February 1998. At least two of his ministers felt he was receiving too much criticism about the way he handled the negotiations over Nagorno-Karabakh. Speculation is that public opinion had become so strong over the issue that Ter-Petrossian feared for his life. In a hastily scheduled election in March 1998, Kocharian won the presidency of Armenia.

With the parliamentary election in 1999, former defense minister Vazgen Sarkissian became prime minister. Karen Demirchian, who had lost to Kocharian in the presidential election in March 1998, became parliamentary speaker. Some people felt that the rise of Sarkissian and Demirchian ultimately would bring about the resignation of Kocharian.

Instead of ousting Kocharian, however, Sarkissian, Demirchian, and several other parliament and cabinet members were killed in a shooting in October 1999. Several gunmen burst into the parliament building and held national-assembly members hostage for several hours, demanding they be allowed to read a statement on national television.

The motive behind the shootings remains unclear. The gunmen's televised statement simply said that the attack was a patriotic action because the government was following ruinous economic and political policies. However, political observers across the world speculate that Sarkissian was hoping to take a stronger position on the Nagorno-Karabakh issue than Kocharian liked. Many Armenians believe the shootings were the result of a conspiracy, in which Kocharian was involved. They note that some of Kocharian's main political rivals at the time were among those killed.

To the public, in turn, the message was clear. Just days before presidential elections in February 2003, Armenian citizens overwhelmingly agreed that the government was not honest and could not be trusted. However, Kocharian secured re-election on March 5, 2003, amid alle-

ARMENIA AND RUSSIA'S SPECIAL RELATIONSHIP

Armenia and Russia have maintained a special relationship throughout the 20th century and going into the 21st century. In part because of animosity against the Turks, Armenians have viewed Russia as their protector. This has continued throughout the Nagorno-Karabakh crisis. For example, Russia shipped more than $1 billion in arms to Armenia from 1993 to 1995. Russian border guards also help patrol Armenia's frontier.

Under the Russian Empire, Armenians were among the ethnic groups that enjoyed trading privileges. That also has continued through various treaties. In the fall of 1993, for example, Russia and Armenia signed an updated friendship treaty as well as a deal to create a joint venture with Gazprom of Russia to supply Armenia with natural gas. In addition, Russia has made it easy for Armenians to gain working visas in their country.

Finally, in mid-July 2002, Armenia signed a pact to eliminate $98 million of debt by turning over five state-owned businesses to Russia. The deal mostly includes high-tech operations that will, in turn, boost Armenia's industrial sector. Even more important, it means Russia will have a meaningful stake in ensuring that Armenia's economy and political stability improve.

Robert Kocharian's reelection to the presidency of Armenia in 2003 was surrounded with allegations of vote fraud, which drew criticism from other European countries and the United States. (Courtesy Armenian Embassy)

gations of massive vote fraud. The election drew severe criticism from European countries and the United States, and diminished Armenia's international stature.

At the same time, these allegations gave Armenians a chance to show their concern about other issues. Thousands of demonstrators took to the streets in late May 2003 in part to show support for opposition candidates but also to give voice to their rage over the broader issue of social inequality. Crime and corruption remain high. Unemployment is still rising, wages are falling, and more people are leaving the country in search of work.

Economy

Armenia's economy has had a very difficult time since its independence. Agricultural output declined by two-thirds from 1991 to 1993 and industrial output was essentially down to nothing in 1992 because of the restructuring after the breakup of the Soviet Union and the ongoing dispute with Azerbaijan that effectively cut off the country's energy supplies. Nearly two-thirds of the population was unemployed in 1993, while inflation hit 30 percent by 1995.

The economy was further crippled by the lingering effects of the 1988 earthquake in Spitak. As late as 2001, nearly 200,000 displaced people needed homes and jobs while the large area surrounding the earthquake needed a completely new infrastructure, including buildings and roads. As a result, foreign aid and the limited tax money received had to be funneled in that direction.

Another 300,000 refugees from Nagorno-Karabakh and other areas of Azerbaijan had to flee their country to live in Armenia because they opposed the Azerbaijani rule of the Armenian enclave. Many of these people have moved to larger towns and the capital, Yerevan, seeking work, housing, and humanitarian aid. As the country struggles to provide them with the basic necessities of life, it is taking away money that could have been used to help build the economy.

The Nagorno-Karabakh crisis has created other economic problems as well. The country has spent millions of dollars in military support when it could have been using the money to help boost other economic sectors. At the same time, it lost precious time developing trade agreements with countries such as the United States. Finally, it has discouraged intercountry projects, such as the development of the Baku-Tbilisi-Ceyhan oil pipeline, which runs from the Azerbaijani coast on the Caspian Sea to the Georgian Black Sea coast. (Armenia could have negotiated to have a link to the pipeline but delayed its decisions so long it was no longer possible by the time the pipeline began construction.)

Add to this a significant amount of economic emigration. Since 1990, more than 500,000 people, or a total of one-fifth the pre-1990 population, have fled the country either because they lost their homes in the 1988 earthquake or for economic reasons. Most of these people immigrated to Russia, the United States, France, and Lebanon.

At the same time, these expatriots also provide a substantial resource for many Armenians. Every year, they send about $250 million to relatives and friends in the country, slightly less than half the country's annual budget. While Armenia claims it would like its citizens to return, the truth is that the country's people would fall into further poverty if they did.

ENERGY

Because Armenia is landlocked and has few energy resources, it must turn to other nations for natural gas and petroleum. Much of these resources used to come from Azerbaijan and Turkey. As a result of bad relations with these neighboring countries, Armenia has had a severe energy shortage, compounded by the fact that the winters of 1996 and 1997 were extremely harsh. Many people had no heating fuel at all and others had just one or two hours of heat and electricity a day.

People turned to burning everything they could find. In the cities today, concrete park benches are still missing their wooden seats. In the countryside, forests that used to cover more than 11 percent of the country are now completely devastated, leaving the country with no wood and no forest habitat for wildlife.

In order to provide much-needed energy to most of the country, the state restarted an old, dilapidated nuclear power plant in the northern town of Metzamor. Unfortunately, the power plant was restarted without adequate safety and backup systems. Russia and the United States stepped in to make the power plant safe, but the concern is that it sits on land that is extremely volatile. It is very likely that if an earthquake hits the region, the power plant will collapse. Fearing this, the international community encouraged Armenia to close the power plant by 2004 and search for an alternative energy source.

TRADE

As they deal with this concern, the country also is working to rebuild its trade network. Under the old Soviet central planning system, Armenia had developed a modern industrial sector supplying manufactured goods to sister republics in exchange for raw materials and energy. This created an artificial trade system for Armenia. Products were manufactured using imported materials. In turn, they were sent to countries that did not have a choice but to accept the Armenian-made goods.

Now that Armenia is independent, its leaders are finding that the cost to import raw materials for manufacturing operations is more than the world's consumers will pay for the finished goods. And, with the economic blockade in place, the country has even fewer outlets for its goods.

The economic blockade by Turkey and Azerbaijan also is hurting the country's trade deficit. Although they can reach Europe and Russia by going through Georgia, and they can reach the Middle East by going through Iran, the roads in these areas are very unreliable, so shipping must be done by expensive air travel. In 1995, fueled by the blockade, the gross domestic product, or the worth of products produced in the country, fell by 60 percent to less than $1 billion.

INDUSTRY

Armenia's biggest concern in terms of its economy is how to develop its industry. Huge defunct factories around the country are a legacy of the former Soviet system. Before the collapse of the Soviet Union, Armenia provided machine-building tools, textiles, and other manufactured goods to neighboring republics in exchange for raw materials and energy. An educated and machine-skilled labor force used to make clothing, washing machines, glass, electronics, automobiles, building supplies, chemicals, and electric motors, among other things. The Soviet Union built upon this base and modernized the factories, but the country's economy is not yet in a position to use that infrastructure.

The country's leaders immediately began to privatize the businesses after the country claimed independence, but the effort has had mixed results. On the one hand, the country refused to privatize industries such as telecommunications, despite urging by foreign aid providers such as the United States. On the other hand, there are few Armenians with the money to invest in large industrial operations that may have an uncertain future.

Much of the reason for the slow move to privatization is the uncertainty about the energy crisis. The factories could be owned by individuals but that does not necessarily mean they can produce anything. The economic blockade with Turkey and Azerbaijan has left very little fuel for running factories—most towns have just a couple of hours of electricity a day—and there remains the question of who is going to buy the goods. The lack of markets to replace those lost in the collapse of the Soviet Union took a major toll on the country's industry, while internal markets dried up because most people are unemployed or underemployed.

Foreign aid has helped little. The United States, for example, has given Armenia more than $1 billion in assistance, second only to that received by Israel, yet every day chronic unemployment is forcing many Armenians to leave the country in search of work.

AGRICULTURE

The Soviet Union had instituted large agro-industrial complexes to increase agricultural production in Armenia. When the country claimed independence, its leaders returned the land to individual farmers. Leaders thought that agriculture would be a major part of the economy to rely on while the industry recovered.

However, agriculture soon began to suffer many of the same problems as industry. With no fuel for tractors and other equipment, and no money to buy fertilizer and pesticides, agricultural production plummeted. With a poor populace, the few food items that were produced frequently rotted in their storage containers. And, with poor, unpredictable roads and rail lines through Georgia and Iran, it was nearly impossible to send the produce outside the country.

In 2003, the country was still not meeting its own needs for foodstuffs. It exported no fresh food items, and more than 10 percent of its imports were vegetables. It is likely that shortage will continue because of the lack of arable land in Armenia. The only notable exception is the liquor industry. Armenia is noted for the quality of its fruits, and grapes grown near Yerevan are made into well-regarded brandy and liqueurs.

Although Armenia must still import much of its foodstuffs, agriculture has always been an important part of the economy. Fruit production occurs in lush mountain valleys. (Robert Kurkjian)

At the same time, pollution is a major concern. Much of the land is contaminated with cancer-causing chemicals such as DDT, leftovers of Soviet efforts to increase the agricultural output of the country.

NEW ECONOMIC SECTORS

In addition to providing aid, foreign countries also are bringing their businesses to Armenia, with the United States leading the way. Approximately 70 U.S.-owned firms currently do business in Armenia, including such multinational corporations as Procter & Gamble, M&M-Mars, Xerox, Dell, and IBM. Recent major U.S. investment projects include the Hotel Armenia, the Hotel Ani, a Greek-owned Coca-Cola bottling plant, petroleum exploration by the American-Armenian Exploration Company, a large perlite mining and processing plant, and a mineral-water production facility.

As the country's leaders works to clean up the industrial and agricultural pollution in its land and water, they are encouraging business people to focus even more on tourism. Although Lake Sevan was lowered during Soviet rule to produce hydroelectric power, plans are being considered to bring the lake up to previous levels and create a resort community on its shores once alternative energy sources are found. Its few mountain resorts also are looking to expand their trade as high-end ski resorts.

Yet another key aspect of Armenia's future is education. While it has a long tradition of education, the country's leaders realize that must continue. It is working with aid dollars to ensure that access to education does not falter during these difficult economic times.

As a side benefit, the leaders also realize that higher education is a product not restricted by geographic location. Armenia's major university in Yerevan already is well-regarded in specific areas such as mining. However, by continuing to build the reputation of the university, Armenia can attract some of the world's brightest people, who, in turn, will help shape Armenia's future.

Health care and other human services are another key growth industry for Armenia's future. Although it is difficult to grow these industries until a population reaches a high enough standard of living to demand them, the country is planning ahead for that day. It is educating health-care workers and earmarking foreign aid to build hospitals.

Throughout all these efforts lies a shadow of concern. Already the country has fallen into the same trap that affects Russia: A high level of organized crime and drug trafficking is replacing legitimate business as an industry. In the first decade after the breakup of the Soviet Union, Armenia saw a sharp increase in drug-related crimes as well as crime in general.

In addition to the obvious social problems organized crime and drug trafficking bring, they also result in the rise of a gray market that can ultimately decimate the country's economic structure. In a gray-market economy, scarce goods are sold for whatever price they will bring. In theory, that sounds like a free-market economy that should help stabilize prices. However, in a struggling economy such as that in Armenia, a gray

GEOGRAPHY CREATES A TURN FOR THE WORSE

The same geography that created the rise of Armenia now contributes to its economic problems. As a remote location, Armenia has few advantages in the industrial sector. As a result, the country's entrepreneurs are being encouraged to develop businesses that are independent of location, such as service bureaus for computer networks or manufacturing small electronic components. The idea is to produce products that are small and thus easy to transport by air or to offer services that can be done through computerized networks.

Recognizing that world trade has developed to a point that Armenia will never be able to recapture its position as a central point for land-based trade, foreign governments and agencies providing aid to Armenia also are encouraging the country's business people to start industries that take advantage of the country's few natural resources. Increased mining for industrial and precious materials, prepared foods, and jewelry making thus have become popular new businesses in Armenia.

In addition to aid, the European Union, Russia, and the United States have signed generous trade agreements that allow Armenian imports with little or no tariffs. As a result, at the end of the year 2001, more than three-fourths of Armenia's exports went to countries that were outside the former Soviet Union. In keeping with the strategy to use the country's resources, more than 40 percent of these exports were precious stones and jewelry, while nearly 15 percent were minerals and precious metals.

market results in high inflation, more crime (to obtain the goods to sell), and greater poverty for the people who do not have the money to buy the goods they need.

THE FUTURE ECONOMY

Although Armenia's economic indicators have risen in recent years, the country still has a long way to go before it is stable and strong. The numbers show that the economy has grown at a steady 4 to 6 percent a year since 1996, and inflation has stabilized at less than 1 percent a year. However, those numbers are misleading. Most of the population is unemployed or severely underemployed, and much of the reported economic growth has come from simply adding foreign aid into the numbers.

Armenia still imports $542 million in products every year, but exports are up from nothing in 1992 to $525 million in 2001. As a result, the dram, Armenia's currency, has stabilized after several years of rapid inflation. In 2002 the country's GDP was estimated at $12.6 billion, although more than one-third of this was from industrial production that could not have been obtained without foreign aid.

The economy has a long way to go to recapture its exuberance of the 1980s. By the end of 1998, Armenia had accrued $800 million in foreign debt, and the economy continues to remain dependent on foreign aid. Most of the population relies heavily on remittances from relatives abroad and remains underemployed. Living conditions remain far below those of the 1980s: Hot water, central heat, cooking fuel, and electricity are not yet available 24 hours a day in all parts of the country. Most of the water is undrinkable due to agricultural and industrial pollution. And even though Armenia's stores have plenty of consumer goods on the shelves, the lack of well-paying jobs keeps those goods on the shelves.

Religion and Culture

Religion and culture are synonymous in Armenia. More than 95 percent of the population is Christian and most of those people belong to the Armenian Church, also known as the Armenian Apostolic Orthodox Church. The country has a small number of Roman Catholics and representatives from other Christian religions, but they represent just 5 percent of the Christian population and are such small groups they do not impose on the dominance of the Armenian Church. The remaining 5 percent of the population is dispersed between nomadic religions, Muslims, and atheists.

Even more important than the dominance of the Armenian Church is its strength. Through 1,800 years of history and dozens of conquerors that tried to convert the people to different religions, the Armenian Church always survived. It developed as a symbol of collective identity for Armenia.

THE ARMENIAN CHURCH

The Armenian Orthodox Church (commonly called the Armenian Church) is a fascinating blend of Christianity and pagan rituals. Because it was founded so early in Christian history, in 301, many historians speculate that it was not really the will of the people, that the adoption of Christianity as the state religion was imposed by the leader at the time, King Tiridates III (r.c. 287–318 or 330).

The Armenian Church continued to allow many pagan rituals in its services, and even today it practices two rituals related to early pagan practices. At various special holy days, Armenians will sacrifice live animals to God as a way to show their adoration. The meat is then distributed to the poor people. Another religious custom involves tying a piece of one's own clothing to a holy tree near a famous church as a sign of your faith and belief that prayers will be answered.

Prior to the adoption of Christianity, most people in the area worshiped the sun god Mithra and Malek Tavous, his representative on Earth. Yezidism, still practiced today by about 60,000 Yezdi people, who reside mostly in the isolated Aragats and Hoktemberian highland areas, was influenced by this ancient religion and continues some of its practices today. Although this sun worship was supplanted by Christianity, most of the first Christian churches were actually built on old temples used to worship Mithra and Malek Tavous.

The mark of early Christianity is nearly everywhere in Armenia. While few of the country's conquerors bothered with the common people, many tried to purge the devout Christians from the area by killing the priests and monks. As a result, the heavy, tall stone walls surrounding ancient churches and monasteries tell the story of a small Christian country that has been continually invaded by hostile neighbors of other denominations.

In spite of this, the Armenian Church was able to conserve many of its ancient churches. Armenia is famed for its church architecture, in which domes are placed above large central spaces. This is considered a marvel of architecture because it was a problem even the Greeks had a difficult time solving 1,000 years ago. Because they are made of hard volcanic stone from the area, the churches are strong enough to survive time and even war. The stone also allowed the churches to be built very large. The oldest churches are more than 1,500 years old and are some of the largest in the world from that time period.

The stone also is ideal for producing intricate carvings. As a result, the interiors of the churches have many large, precise geographic carvings accented with shades of brown dye. These include intricate maps of the larger geographic area, as well as drawings of individuals streets and small villages. Most of the churches do not have paintings, frescoes, or stained glass. The altar is raised like a stage, possibly as a compromise to the people's pagan roots.

During the Soviet Union's anti-religion period, beginning in the 1920s, most of the Armenian priests were killed and religious artifacts were destroyed. (Many, of course, were hidden in the caves in the mountains or in people's homes.) People who spoke for Christianity were imprisoned, and church services could not be held. Interestingly, the Armenian Church was not deterred by this and remained a strong force in people's lives. Religious leaders held private services in secret, and people gathered in each other's homes to pray. Eventually, the Soviet Union even called on the church to help rally people to fight in World War II.

The Soviet Union also forbade any artists, musicians, and writers to produce religious works. Works that already had been produced were either destroyed or forbidden to be used.

The Armenia Orthodox Church is extremely conservative as compared to Western religions, which the monks and priests consider dangerously liberal. Similar to the Russian Orthodox Church, the Armenian Orthodox Church uses its own liturgical calendar, celebrating events such as Easter and Christmas at times other than Catholic and Protestant Churches. The priests dress in elaborate vestments and gilded icons are frequently used in services. They use an early translation of the Bible that pre-dates the King James version by several centuries. As a legacy of the Soviet period, many churches do not hold regular services. People rarely receive sacraments in the churches—such as marriage or even baptism—and often only gather for specific Christian holy days such as Easter and Christmas. In the last decade, though, some churches have become increasingly popular as pilgrimage sites for Armenians. Most of these are churches that have cultural significance, such as the home to a famous Christian author, or are reputed to be the site of miracles.

CULTURE

Given the importance of the Armenian Church for the national consciousness, it is no surprise that most of Armenia's cultural tradition stems from its Christian roots.

Armenians are very proud of the long artistic tradition in their country. Art that was distinctively Armenian in form first emerged in the early

ST. GREGORY OF NAREK

St. Gregory of Narek (950–1003) is revered as the greatest figure of medieval Armenian religious thought and literature. He came from a family of religious scholars—his father was a bishop and his uncle an abbot of the monastery of Narek. Gregory quickly surpassed them when he studied everything from music and literature to astronomy and geometry at the monastery. He wrote discourses, poems, chants, doxologies, and commentaries. Many of his works are included in the Divine Liturgy celebrated each Sunday in Armenian churches.

His most famous work, however, is *The Book of Lamentations*, containing 95 chapters united under the theme of "Conversations with God from the depths of the heart." The book tries to put into words the sighs of the broken and contrite heart. It is considered a "new" book of psalms that encompasses the range of human frailty and emotions. It seeks to guide its readers toward reconciliation with God through a series of all-embracing prayers, rich in imagery, and resonating with Biblical allusions.

The book is said to have special healing powers, especially Prayer 18. As a result, *The Book of Lamentations* often is placed under the pillow of a sick person.

fourth century A.D., coinciding with the introduction of Christianity. Religious icons were favored subjects during that time. Historically, Armenia subsequently had three major artistic periods, which coincided with periods of independence or semi-independence.

The classical period, from the fourth to the seventh centuries, was the first, formative period of Armenian art and literature. It started with the conversion to Christianity and ended with the Arab invasion and occupation of Armenia. During this time, distinctive, elaborate stonework and metalwork evolved as well as religious writings.

The 10th and 11th centuries, under the patronage of the Bagratid kings, saw a return to the older art forms but also was a time when artists experimented with new forms, such as frescoes, woodworking, and intricate paintings depicting religious scenes.

The Bagratid dynasty provided the security essential for the flourishing of art, architecture, and the construction of large monastic complexes. From the 12th century to the 14th, a new renaissance, encouraged and patronized by large noble families, gave Armenian art its last creative moment. The result was many of the large churches and other structures still in use today.

Music

The country is most famous for its classical music, with several famous composers from the 20th century. The country's two most famous composers are Aram Khatchaturian (1903–78) and Soghomon Soghomonian (better known as Komitas). Khatchaturian researched the country's disappearing folk music tunes, then composed classical music for piano and orchestra. His works include several short pieces for piano, including the well-known "Sabre Dance" and the ballet *Spartacus*. The Christian monk Komitas was taken by the Turks to look at his dead compatriots in the great slaughter of 1915. After that he vowed never to write music again and went to a Paris hospital, where he died in 1939.

Music is very important to Armenians, and every family except the most poor teaches its children at least one musical instrument, most commonly the piano. Folk music is popular, taking its tunes from a mixture of Russian, Iranian, and Turkish influences. Likewise, folk dances emulate the circular dances of these three nations and often include just one sex dancing at a time.

THE MADONNA OF ARMENIA

Nune Yesayan is an Armenian singer known for her fusion of traditional Armenian folk songs with jazz and pop music. Her concerts feature nationalistic songs with traditional instruments such as *duduk* and *saz* vying for space with keyboards, guitars, and trumpets.

The 29-year-old Yesayan also produces spectacular events accompanied by male and female dancers. One concert started with the performers moving through the audience in the lobby, passing out fruit, juggling, and generally producing the atmosphere of an old Armenian city. These events have given her the European nickname "The Madonna of Armenia."

In recent years, she also has become popular in the United States. In May 1998, for example, she performed at sold-out concerts in San Francisco and Pasadena, California. She also used some of the profits from a European concert to help the victims of the September 11, 2001, attack on New York's World Trade Center.

As with many stars, Yesayan's life has not been easy. Coming from a traditional family, she was not encouraged to become a performer, so she entered an engineering school after high school. She later was accepted into a music college when she met people who supported her talent. Yesayan also married an Armenian man who insisted she give up singing and convinced her that she had no talent. After one year, she separated from him and started singing again.

Her albums include *Ov Inch Kidi (Who Knows . . .?)*, *Kavarn Mer (Our Small Village)*, and *Ashkharah (The World)*. Much of her concert profits go to the All-Armenia Fund for helping impoverished Armenians.

Painting and Sculpture

The fine arts of painting and sculpture also are alive in Armenia. Contemporary painter Arvand Kochar has his own gallery filled with portraits. Now living in Moscow, he is famous for this graphics work. Minas Avetisian is another well-known recent painter in Armenia, although his work was neglected during the Soviet realist art period because it was less realistic than the Soviets demanded.

Martiros Sarian, on the other hand, was a painter of realistic works and one of Armenia's most famous artists from the Soviet period. His house in Yerevan is filled with photos, along with bold and colorful landscapes, portraits, and still lifes. During Soviet times, many travelers would come to Armenia just to see his works.

Armenia continues to encourage its artists. A Sarian sculpture in Sarian Park in Yerevan is home on the weekends to a burgeoning contemporary art scene, where painters gather to offer a critique of each other's work and sell their paintings. Most of the paintings have religious iconography or capture familiar Armenia landscapes.

Film

Armenian film director Sergei Parajanov (1924–1990) was ostracized under the former Soviet system for not following the style of official Soviet realist art. But even without official support, Parajanov managed to create several films—*Color of Pomegranates* (1969), *Legend of Suram Fortress* (1985) and *Ashik Kerib* (1988)—which gained him respect among the leading film producers and directors of the 1960s.

Literature

An Armenian literary tradition first emerged in the fifth century. Literary themes were at first historical or religious, as represented by two great works of the period, *The History of Armenia,* by Movses Khorenatsi and Eznik Kohgbatsi's *Refutation of the Sects.* The first great Armenian poet was the 10th-century bishop St. Gregory of Narek, whose mystical poems and hymns strongly influenced the Armenian Apostolic Church; his works are only now being translated into English (see sidebar).

Literature developed only after annexation by Russia when dissidents began to write about their love of Armenia and called for a separation from the Soviet Union. The best-known novelist from this time is Hakob Melik-Hakobian (1835–88), known as Raffi. His works were banned during the Soviet era, although most Armenians read at least excerpts from his many works during that time. Today his works remain popular as they fuel the population's new nationalism.

Writer Khachatur Abovian (1805–48) is known as Armenia's answer to Chaucer for his poetry and works, including *Armenia's Wounds,* about the genocide of Armenians in the early 1900s. The author is also known for adding a few more letters to the alphabet to make it more useful to Armenians trying to learn foreign languages. Unfortunately, it is hard to find many books for sale in Armenia because most were destroyed in the Soviet era, and the country has yet to rebuild a publishing industry. Very few books have been translated into English.

Folk Art

As with any very old culture, Armenia has a rich tradition of folk art that has remained unchanged throughout the centuries. Armenians are known for their beautiful textiles featuring pastel fabrics with elaborate white embroidery. Their rugs have a distinctly Turkish look but feature more Christian symbols in the weaving. The Nagorno-Karabakh region is especially famous for its intricately woven carpets. Woodworking and metalwork both feature elaborate geometric designs, while the volcanic rock is still used to carve decorative stone monuments called *khatchkars*.

Because of religious persecution by the Turks and then the Soviets, many of the country's artists chose to leave for Europe or the United States. Well-known contemporary Armenian writer William Saroyan (1908–81) lived in the United States most of his life. The great Armenian painter Arshile Gorky (1904–48), one of the first generation of abstract expressionists, went to the United States after his mother starved to death in the Turkish massacre of Armenians.

Sports

Armenia has shown some modest success in international sports competition, in part because it is still a very poor country. Its soccer team has participated in the qualifying round in the World Cup and other international tournaments. It also has had some success with wrestling and gymnastics at the Olympic level.

While children play soccer, basketball, and tennis after school, men tend to play chess or backgammon in the park. Both of these games are very popular pastimes and are learned at a very young age.

Both young and old enjoy watching sports. The most popular events are soccer matches and basketball games.

Daily Life

Daily life for most Armenians revolves around family, religion, and hard work. What little time is left over at the end of a busy day usually is spent relaxing with family and friends or, if money is available, going to a cultural event such as the ballet or a classical concert.

Housing is in very short supply thanks to the influx of Armenian refugees from Azerbaijan and the 200,000 people still homeless from the 1988 earthquake. As a result, most Armenians live in an apartment that Americans would consider very small. They likely live with at least one set of grandparents and often some aunts, uncles, and cousins. This means there is very little privacy. People sleep in the living room and several children will share not just a bedroom but even a bed. Overnight guests also are common, as distant relatives come to visit or to stay while they look for work.

The typical Armenian family lives in the capital city of Yerevan or in one of the small towns dotting the country. Even those who work in agriculture frequently live in small villages instead of on isolated farmsteads, although people in the smaller towns are more likely to have individual houses than apartments. The parents will both work, if they can both find jobs, and the grandparents or other elderly family member will take care of the household and young children.

Luxuries are rare in Armenia since the breakup of the Soviet Union. Many families may own an older car, but it is seldom used for daily transportation. Instead, the children and parents will either walk to school and work or they will take public transportation. Fuel prices are still very high because of the embargo on natural gas and petroleum by Turkey and Azerbaijan. As a result, the automobile is used only for emergencies.

Larger towns have adequate train or bus routes that take most people within a few blocks of their final destinations. Public transportation also remains inexpensive—about 25 cents a trip—thanks in large part to the Soviet days when subsidized public transportation was mandatory.

PARENTS

Being an adult in Armenia today is to be a busy worrier. One worries about one's job, one's family's health, and whether one will be able to supply basic needs. It is very likely that both parents aspire to work outside the home, since, under the Soviet system, they would both have been required to work. In addition, Armenians are a very hard-working culture, so the wife would naturally want to contribute to her family's standard of living.

However, since the breakup of the Soviet Union, jobs have been very hard to find. Most factory work has evaporated. If the father of the family was a factory foreman or a skilled laborer in the factory, today he might be selling bananas on a street corner or driving a taxicab. Likewise, the mother, who might have been trained as an engineer, today might be working as a janitor or doing manual labor in a mine.

The parents also might be trying to start a new business in one of the many areas that are receiving financial aid from foreign countries, such as jewelry making. Most parents also have part-time jobs on the evenings and weekends. They may take in laundry, sell items on the gray or black markets, run a café, drive a taxi, or clean the homes of wealthier people. In other words, they will be focusing all their energies on making as much money as they can in a difficult economy.

Armenians tend to wear conservative clothing. The women almost always wear skirts that cover their knees with basic blouses and sweaters. The men wear dark pants and basic cotton shirts. Shorts, tank tops, and miniskirts are almost never seen on the streets, even among adolescents.

THE GRANDPARENTS

The grandparents in an Armenian family play a very important role. Not only do they baby-sit the young children, they also run the household. The grandmother likely does most of the housework, which is a very challenging job when there is little hot water and sometimes no electricity.

If she has the money, the grandmother will do other shopping. She also will stop at the post office, where she will, hopefully, pick up some money sent to her from a relative in a foreign country. If she does receive money, she will take it to the bank to have it converted into *drams*, the local currency. She also might spend several hours sitting outside the family's apartment building trying to sell her meager belongings, or she will take a part-time job cleaning others' apartments.

While the grandmother is doing these errands, the grandfather may be trying to repair items around the house, such as the stove or the radio. By now, these items are several decades old and the family almost certainly can not afford new ones yet. The house or apartment has wood heat, so he will keep the fire stoked in the winter and possibly go out hunting for more wood to burn. He also will go to one of several spots in town that have pure water so he can fill up the family's water jugs. If he has extra time before heading home, he might stop at the park and play a game of chess with his friends.

In the evening, grandfather may teach the family's sons metalworking or woodworking, while grandmother will pass on many of the recipes she learned to cook from her own grandmother.

Although the grandmother and grandfather have important roles in the family, they do not make all the decisions. The husband and wife who bring in the majority of the income will be deferred to on most occasions. They will ask the grandparents for advice on how to spend the money but do not always follow that advice. At this point in their lives, even if the grandparents own the home that the extended family is living in, they are just happy to have family members to take care of them.

Difficult economic times demand that the elderly find ways to make money if no one can care for them. At Garni, these roadside vendors sell apples to support themselves. (Facts On File, Inc.)

WHAT THEY EAT

Although Armenia is a Christian country, its food has definite Islamic roots. The food is very spicy and often contains a lot of garlic. People often eat shish kebabs of lamb cooked over open fires. Stews such as *solyanka* are made of beef hocks, ears, and other remnants heavily spiced with herbs such as coriander, tarragon, and paprika. Yogurt is very popular but is used more as an addition to a dish than eaten alone as it is in the United States and Europe. The yogurt is often mixed with mint and used to thicken and flavor soups.

Although many different fruits are eaten fresh in Armenia, one of the favorites is *pshat,* the fruit of the oleaster. It is acorn-shaped and has a dry, dusty taste.

The bread, called *lavash,* is much like baklava without the sweetness. It begins as a large, thin sheet of dough and then is folded over again and again.

Drinks are almost always flavored with spices. Several cold drinks are made using tarragon to spice them. Another, called *tahn,* is made with salt and minted yogurt. Most towns have their own wine-making facilities that use local fruits such as mulberry and apricots. Some is distilled to make brandy. The country also makes a number of light and dark beers.

THE CHILDREN

Children are very prized in the Armenian family, although young Armenian couples can not afford to have children yet, so there are very few babies and toddlers in Armenia.

Even in rural communities, children attend school through high school. They start at age five and continue until they graduate, often not until they are 20 years old. In grade school, they study a well-rounded curriculum of science, history, math, and languages. In addition to Armenian, they learn Russian. Children in Yerevan and other large towns also will learn English.

In secondary school, the students will decide where they want to focus their lives. Those chosen to go on to college will pick four to five areas they want to study and will master those before they graduate. If they decide to go to a trade school, they will attend a different high school that

Armenian youths choose a career path by secondary school. These young seminary students will become clergymen in the Armenian Apostolic Church. (Facts On File, Inc.)

focuses on the trades. The emphasis will be on having them enter the workforce as soon as they graduate.

The schools also serve as a place to teach culture. High school students will learn folk dancing, classical dancing, and dining etiquette as part of their regular curriculum.

However, unlike the United States, most Armenian children do not take physical education classes in school. Soccer, basketball, tennis, gymnastics, and wrestling are the most popular sports activities, but they are offered strictly through private organizations. Other activities such as band or drama club also are offered outside of school in the evenings and weekends.

After school, the children come home and complete their homework as well as any family chores. They change into play clothes that are very similar to those worn in the United States. If they have a pet, the animal is very cherished and considered a status symbol, so they take very good care of it. They may take the dog for a walk or let the cat play in their bedroom.

At least one day a week, the children will take piano or violin lessons if the family can afford it. They also may be on an athletic team, in which case they will go to practice after school. The oldest children might have after-school jobs doing menial work such as housecleaning.

FREE TIME

Although most Armenian churches still do not hold services on Sundays, religion is still an important part of life. Prayers are said before meals and before going to bed. The families will attend services on holy days, and they may make pilgrimages to one of the many old churches or monasteries dotting the countryside. Family members will go to church to say individual prayers, and they will mark important anniversaries such as births and deaths by all going to church to light candles and say prayers.

There is no cable television; many of the stations are state-run and broadcast programs that are of little interest to children. As a result, television is not a big part of their lives. They likely do not have computers or games such as PlayStation and Atari. If they do own a computer, it is used for school work and for the family business.

Because the families are large and the house is small, there is little room for toys or even a lot of clothing. As a result, the children usually make up their own games. They may listen to classical or folk music on the one or two radio stations available in their town, but they more likely will go to the park to be with their friends.

If someone new comes into the family's life, such as a foreign visitor or a relative they have not seen in a long time, the person will be treated as if he or she were royalty. The parents might even miss work to take this newcomer to a museum. The children will be asked to give up their bedrooms. A large meal will be served with elaborate toasts and courses of food that can last for hours.

When a special festival is held in town, the children will be dressed in traditional Armenian costumes, with white blouses and colorful skirts for the girls, and white shirts with dark pants and colorful belts and hats for the boys. They will perform traditional circle dances, listen to traditional folk music, and perhaps watch as their parents become nostalgic when a traditional love song is played.

Cities

Although Armenia is an urban country with very few people living on farms, it does not have many large cities. Yerevan, the capital, is the only city with more than 1 million people. Gyumri, with 160,000 people, is the next largest city and sits in the northwest corner of the country. These are the only two cities with airports, so they serve as the nexus for the country's imports and exports. The third largest city, Vanadzor, has 150,000 people.

The remaining small towns are dotted around the country at intervals of 10 to 20 miles and serve as a reminder of the country's roots as a nexus for trade: This is the farthest distance one can reasonably travel with pack animals in one day, so travelers' inns had to be spaced about this far apart. As the country grew, the inns naturally turned into small towns that supported fledgling industries.

YEREVAN

Although it has just 1.1 million people, the city has all the amenities and sights you would expect in the capital of any country. And, because it is relatively small, all these things are within a three-quarter-mile radius from the center of the city. Whether you want to visit a puppet theater, a major medical center, an ancient church, or the sports complex, a short bus ride would take you there.

In the early 1920s, at the request of Soviet rulers, a completely new city was built over most of the old one, which had some sections more than 2,000 years old. The new design was more geometric than the previous hodge-podge that had been built up haphazardly for more than two and a half millennia. It contained preplanned recreation areas and specific areas designated for industry and housing. All the roads radiate from a central town square that also provides easy access to the bus and train.

Yerevan also is a study in contrasts between old Armenia and the new world economy. On one street, you might find a Yum Yum Donut shop and a Pizza di Roma restaurant nestled between an 11th-century church and an Internet café. Nearly all the buildings are built from off-white volcanic rock. The city has about a dozen hotels and nearly 50 museums of every size and subject matter. It also is home to the country's opera house

YEREVAN PREDATES ROME

Yerevan was founded in 782 B.C. (nearly 30 years before Rome was founded), when King Argishti, a recent conqueror of the area, decided to build his fortress at the crossroads of several trade routes. He had his builders write on a tablet at the site, "With the power of Khaldi, I, Argishti, son of Menu, erected this stronghold and named it Erebuni to the glory of the country of Biaina and to the fear of its enemies." The tablet can still be viewed today in one of the city's museums.

Before the country was carved into its current small size, Yerevan actually was more centrally located. As a result, it often served as a battleground for conquering armies and remained the hub of the country's economic activity. With each conquest came new churches, homes, and business places, many of which are still visible today.

It is no wonder that conquerors often decided to stay in the city. Yerevan sits in a valley ringed on three sides by hills so it was difficult for approaching armies to reach. To the southwest, it opens onto the Urartian Plain, which offers spectacular views of Mount Ararat. Although much of the ancient area was destroyed when the Soviet Union rebuilt the city, many areas still contain the ancient flavor.

and every kind of shopping, from open-air markets to expensive Parisian boutiques.

Yerevan is home to most of the country's large industrial complexes, only a few of which are in the central part of the city. For the most part, the industry is set up in areas on the northwest and southwest edges of the town to take advantage of the Hrazdan River for dumping waste products. Many of the factories, most of which were built under Soviet rule, are vacant today.

GYUMRI

Gyumri was almost completely destroyed by the 1988 earthquake. At that time, it had 250,000 people. More than 18,000 were killed, and most of the rest were left homeless. As a result, the northwestern-most city in Armenia has dwindled to almost half its 1988 size.

The Gyumri airport still runs a few flights each day, but the town exists more as a matter of tradition than usefulness today. It used to be the last major stop for goods traveling into Turkey and Georgia, so many of the farmers from the Mount Aragats valley brought their items into Gyumri to sell.

In ancient times, Gyumri was an important trading center, probably for traders coming across the mountains through what is now Turkey. It was first mentioned in a cuneiform inscription found at the Marmashen church complex thought to be from the seventh century B.C., and Greek historian Xenophon included the city in his writings from the seventh and sixth centuries B.C.

Currently, there is little to see in Gyumri. There are a few museums and ancient churches, as well as a 19th-century Russian fortress. The ruins from the earthquake have yet to be rebuilt and may not be for many years, as most of the people whose homes and workplaces were destroyed have moved to other cities by now.

In between Gyumri and Yerevan lies Mount Aragats, the highest mountain currently in Armenia, at about 14,000 feet. Ashtarak, the closest town of any size, has 20,000 people. It is known for its heavy wine but actually is more interesting for its old structures. It has a fifth-century church and bridge, as well as many monuments and tombs. It also has a 13th-century church. The small town-fortress of Ambered was constructed during the reign of Kamsarid in the seventh century to protect their kingdom from invaders. At more than 7,000 feet above sea level, on the slopes of Mt. Aragats, the fortress has views over the Urartian Plan.

VANADZOR

Vanadzor is the third-largest town in Armenia, with a population of about 150,000. Its name means "The Beauty of Lori," referring to the region of the country in which it is located. The town was greatly damaged in the 1988 earthquake. Although the area is being rebuilt, most of the old churches have been lost.

GARNI

Although it has just a few thousand people, the town of Garni, about 15 miles east of Yerevan, is one of the most important to the country's history. It was an ancient summer resident of Armenian kings and has been inhabited since at least the eighth century B.C.

Although many of the ancient buildings have been destroyed by earthquakes and newer construction, the original site of the summer home is still interesting. It contains the ruins of a 1,000-foot high tower and a three-sided fortress with 14 towers. A temple built by the Romans in the first century A.D. and dedicated to the Roman sun god Helios was reconstructed in the 1960s. Inside the temple is a restored fire pit, possibly used for sacrifices.

A Roman bathhouse is still on the grounds, as well as a seventh-century church. Both contain stones with interesting sayings. In the bathhouse, for example, is a Greek saying, "We worked, but did not get anything." In the church, an eighth-century-B.C. stone says, "Argishti, son of Menua, took people and cattle from Garni to Erebuni to create a new community."

LAKE SEVAN REGION

Several small towns lie on the banks of Lake Sevan, or within a couple of miles of the lake. Many of them began their lives in ancient times as trading stations and inns for travelers. Sevan, the town, sits at the north end of the hills that ring the lake, and although it has a nice setting, it is primarily an industrial town. It has only 10,000 people, and there is little to see except vacationers hanging out on the rocky shores of the lake in the summer.

The nearby towns of Dilijan and Ijevan are surrounded by steep mountains and pine forests. These towns are close to some of the ancient ruins found in the 1950s, when the Soviets lowered the lake for hydroelectric power and irrigation. They also are set in beautiful areas, so have a strong history as vacation spots. Dilijan also has a small museum of 19th-century Armenian crafts.

Historically, the road leading from Yerevan to Sevan is very interesting. It has many monasteries built in the ninth to 11th centuries. Many of these are set high up in the mountains, surrounded by thick stone walls, and are still maintained as they were a thousand years ago.

NORTHERN ARMENIA

Stepanavan was badly hit in the 1988 earthquake, so about half of the town has been rebuilt. It is the first major town when entering Armenia from the north, although it is not very big and has very little industry today.

Spitak was the epicenter of the 1988 earthquake. It also has had some buildings replaced, such as its hospital and its church. There is little left to the original town, where 4,000 people (about half the inhabitants at the time) were killed in the earthquake. Many of the people living there refused to leave, though, and lived the next few years in shipping containers. They have since built new housing.

SOUTHERN ARMENIA

Armenia's remote southern region is sandwiched between Azerbaijan to the east and the Azerbaijani enclave of Nakhichevan to the west. The city of Goris was named an administrative district of the Russian state in 1870. Meghri, near the Iranian border, is known for its fruit production, especially apricots, and Sisian has a large military base.

NOTES

p. 39 "It has borrowed some words from Persian and Turkish . . ." Buford, Tim. *Georgia with Armenia* (Guilford, Ct.: Globe Pequot Press, 2002), pp. 251–252.

p. 42 "Bagratian resigned his post officially . . ." *The Statesman's Yearbook* (London: Palgrave Macmillan, 2002), p. 51.

p. 45 "The election drew severe criticism . . ." Giragosin, Richard. "The Implications of Armenia's Post-Election Crisis." March 19, 2003. Eurasianet www.eurasianet.org/departments/insight/articles/pp031903.shtml. Downloaded May 2, 2003.

p. 45 "Nearly two-thirds of the population . . ." *The Statesman's Yearbook* (London: Palgrave Macmillan, 2002), p. 50.

p. 63 "Although Armenia is a Christian country, its food has definite Islamic roots . . ." Wilson, Neil. *Georgia, Armenia & Azerbaijan Travel Guide* (New York: Lonely Planet Guide Books, 2002), p. 191.

6
AZERBAIJAN

The Land and Its People

Azerbaijan is the largest of the three Caucasian nations. It is 33,440 square miles in area, about the size of Indiana, although its ragged borders give it a much larger appearance on a map. It is bordered by Russia on the north, Georgia on the northwest, Armenia on the west, Iran on the south, and the Caspian Sea on the east. A small area called Nakhichevan (pronounced Na-Hee-CHEE-Van) also is part of Azerbaijan but it is entirely separated from the rest of the country by Armenian land.

The most interesting feature about Azerbaijan is the Baku peninsula. Home to the country's capital city, Baku, it juts straight into the Caspian Sea for about 30 miles. This creates natural protection for harboring large sea-faring vessels. It also creates a natural staging area for the country's abundant gas and oil reserves that sit just off the coast in the Caspian Sea.

Slightly less than half the land area in Azerbaijan is mountainous. The mountains form a horseshoe shape around the country, with the opening looking out at the Caspian Sea. The Greater Caucasus Mountains in the northeast, the Lesser Caucasus in the southwest, and the Kura River depression in between all converge in Azerbaijan. In addition to the Caucasus Mountains, the Talysh mountains are in the extreme southeast of the country.

With so many mountain chains and a large sea border, Azerbaijan has more different climate areas than any other country its size. Scientists divide the world into 13 different climate zones, and Azerbaijan has nine of these, ranging from humid subtropical to desert to alpine.

Temperatures and rainfall vary dramatically across the country. The mean annual temperature ranges from 59 degrees Fahrenheit in the lowlands to 32 degrees in the mountains. The mean temperatures in July are 79 degrees Fahrenheit in the lowlands and 41 degrees in the highlands. Rainfall is eight to 12 inches in the coastal region and in the southeastern lowlands, 12 to 35 inches in the foothills of the medium-elevation mounts, 39 to 51 inches on the southern slopes of the Greater Caucasus, and 47 to 55 inches in the southern lowland. In the lowland, precipitation falls in the winter, while in the mountains and foothills it falls in the summer.

The result is an amazing variety of plants and wildlife, as well as diverse land for raising crops and animals. The country has more than 4,000 species of plants and more than 12,000 species of animals native to its lands. It also has several hundred types of birds, as well as both freshwater and saltwater fish.

The highest mountains contain many glaciers and fast-flowing rivers, while the mid-level mountains have deep gorges and valleys. The highest peak is Mount Bazardyuzyu (14,652 feet), in the Greater Caucasus on the border with Russia.

As the Greater Caucasus Mountains spread eastward, they get slightly smaller and eventually drop off abruptly, becoming low hills. At this point, the climate is very dry and subtropical. The land continues to get more dry toward the east until it becomes desert near Baku. The average temperature in the summer is just under 80 degrees Fahrenheit, but it is not uncommon for it to reach 104 degrees during the hottest part of the day. The city has virtually no rainfall during the summer months and receives fewer than four inches for the entire year.

Although much of Azerbaijan is desert, the country does not lack for water. Azerbaijan has more than 1,000 rivers coming out the mountains. Most are short—but 21 are longer than 60 miles—yet they contain enough water to irrigate other parts of the country. The Kura is the largest river in the Caucasian countries and flows northwest to southeast. It begins high in the Greater Caucasus Mountains and eventually empties into the Caspian Sea.

Azerbaijan also is dotted with very small lakes. The largest, Lake Hajikabul, is just six square miles and the next largest, Lake Boyukshor, is just four square miles.

SIZE DEPENDS ON THE OBSERVER

Because the area has been conquered many times throughout history, and because the Soviet Union broke some regions of Azerbaijan into autonomous republics, the country's citizens often view parts of the world that are not technically part of their country as being "emotionally" Azerbaijani.

For example, the region of Iran south of the Aras River, which forms the border, is also known as Azerbaijan to many of the older people living in the country. The people on both sides of the border speak the same language and have the same religion. There are technically no territorial disputes, although the two countries disagree on determining their territorial limits in the Caspian Sea.

Likewise, Azerbaijan currently is having a dispute with Armenia over the Nagorno-Karabakh area in the southwest corner of Azerbaijan. Under Soviet rule, the area was considered part of Azerbaijan, but it contains almost exclusively Armenian people. Armenians who live there, as well as the ones who live in Armenia, would like to see the area returned. Part of the area is occupied by Armenian troops, but politically it is still considered part of Azerbaijan.

The large mountain ranges also bring fertile land on their lower slopes. As the mountains rose, they pushed the fertile land outward. These lands are filled with lush pastures and large broad-leaved forests that have a moderate climate much like that of the northern United States. The area is pleasantly warm in the summer yet cold enough in the winter to get large snowfalls.

A broad plain lies in the center "horseshoe" area of the country. While it naturally contains few rivers, irrigation systems were built during Soviet times to bring water from the mountain rivers to create farmland perfect for growing cotton and grain.

The southeastern Talysh region has a humid subtropical climate. It receives more than 50 inches of rain a year. Summer temperatures often reach more than 90 degrees Fahrenheit. Although most of the rain falls in the winter, enough falls in the summer to keep the area extremely humid. As a result, this area of the country is covered with subtropical forests.

The Nagorno-Karabakh region, occupied by Armenians, lies in the southwest. It is blanketed with lush mountain woodlands. The mountains do not get extremely high, so the area does not receive the devastating snowfalls and cold that high mountain peaks receive. Mountain goats, deer, and lynx make their homes among the broadleaved forests.

THE PEOPLE

Azerbaijan has about 7.8 million people, about the same as the state of Michigan. Only little more than half of them live in cities, in large part because much of the land is suitable for farming. Of those who live in cities, about one-third live in the Baku-Sumgait area. About two-thirds of the city dwellers live along the Caspian Sea coast. The inland towns are small and spread far apart.

Ninety percent of the people are native Azerbaijani. Other groups include Russians, Armenians, Turks, Georgians, Ukrainians, Germans, and other nationalities. However, none of these groups have more than 500,000 people living in the entire country.

Many of the minority groups have lived in small groups within the cities or countryside of Azerbaijan for several centuries. Although they could be described as native Azerbaijanis, their close-knit culture and choice of religion usually keep them bonded to their original heritage.

Many Azerbaijanis also are spread around the world. There are nearly 1 million living in Russia and another 400,000 in the United States. More than 18 million ethnic Azerbaijanis live in the Azerbaijan provinces of northern Iran.

Most of the people speak Azerbaijani, a language that is closely related to Turkish. Russian is still taught in the schools, and most adults speak Russian as one of their primary languages. The Azerbaijani language was originally written in Arabic, but in the 1920s, the Roman alphabet (that used in English and European languages) was introduced. In 1939, the Soviet Union demanded that the country switch to using the Cyrillic alphabet (the one used in Russia). After Azerbaijan gained independence, the government adopted yet another alphabet that was a Turkish version of the Roman script.

Nearly all the ethnic Azerbaijanis are Muslim. The religion, Islam, was introduced to the area during the seventh century and was made the official religion of Azerbaijan in the 16th century. However, during Soviet rule, the practice of religion was condemned. The religious leaders were persecuted and the mosques were closed or destroyed.

Since the breakup of the Soviet Union, there has been a revival of the Islamic faith. Mosques have reopened and religious leaders are present again. Saudi Arabia and other Islamic countries have provided financial assistance to promote the Islamic revival in Azerbaijan.

However, this does not mean that Azerbaijan is a religious culture. Most of the people do not actively practice their religion. The majority of the people say prayers a few times a day and honor holy days, but they are not opposed to other religious groups. However, the Muslim, Christian, and Jewish groups rarely mix after working hours. Even in the cities, the ethnic groups tend to live in distinct areas. They rarely marry outside their religious groups.

Unlike Georgia and Armenia, Azerbaijan has a high rate of population growth. The country increased in population by about 2 percent from 1990 to 2000. This could be a result of Azerbaijan's relative wealth as compared with Georgia, and Armenia as a result of the country's abundant oil and gas resources. Nearly half the population work in agriculture, where they can raise their own food and thus afford to have larger families.

Most of the Azerbaijanis can read and write as a result of the Soviet Union's mandatory education system, which has continued after independence, as well. Children must attend at least eight years of school, and most graduate after 10 years. Many go on to attend one of the country's colleges or technical institutes, including Baku State University, Azerbaijan Technical University, and Azerbaijan State Petroleum Academy.

The Government

Azerbaijan declared independence on August 30, 1991. Although the Communist Party was dissolved, the September elections that year named Communist Ayaz N. Mutalibov as president, and most of the party members retained their positions. Mutalibov had been incumbent chairman of the Supreme Soviet and was the sole candidate in Azerbaijan's first direct presidential election. However, it was not until

October 18 that Mutalibov finally implemented the declaration of independence.

In February 1992, Azerbaijan joined with the four Central Asian republics of Kyrgyzstan, Tajikistan, Turkmenistan, and Uzbekistan in gaining admission to the long-dormant Economic Cooperation Organization that had been founded by Iran, Turkey, and Pakistan in 1963. Some, however, viewed the revived grouping as merely alleviating rather than eliminating tensions between fundamentalist Iran and secular Turkey, with Azerbaijan seen as more sympathetic to Turkey. To further strengthen this close relationship, Turkey exerted considerable diplomatic effort to bring about a settlement of the Nagorno-Karabakh conflict that would preserve Azerbaijan's sovereignty over the enclave.

NAGORNO-KARABAKH

Azerbaijan, however, had little chance of winning the war. Their citizens had been used by the Soviet army mostly as construction workers, while Armenia's soldiers had received the best training. Mutalibov also was reluctant to build a strong army because he feared he would not have enough control over it.

In March, 1992, the town of Khojali in Nagorno-Karabakh fell to Armenian forces, and many Azerbaijani civilians were massacred. The Azerbaijani people formed angry demonstrations in Baku to protest, and, by May 15, Mutalibov was ousted.

On June 7, Abulfaz Ali Elchibey, a former dissident and political prisoner, defeated four competitors in a new round of presidential balloting. He advocated closer relations with Iran and Turkey, and opposed Azerbaijan's membership in the Commonwealth of Independent States (CIS), a loose-unit organization of former Soviet republics.

Elchibey and his Armenian counterpart immediately began negotiations to find a solution to the Nagorno-Karabakh problem. However, in a public vote, virtually all the Armenians in Nagorno-Karabakh, the overwhelming majority of the population, voted for independence.

The situation began to worsen. Armenia enforced a blockade of Nakhichevan, the small, separated region of Azerbaijan located on the western border of Armenia. In return, Azerbaijan prohibited any goods to enter Armenia from Azerbaijan. It also enlisted Turkey as an ally in the

Azerbaijan president Heydar Aliyev (center) was elected with 98.8 percent of the vote, but supporters worry about his failing health and its possible effects on the nation's leadership. (Courtesy NATO)

blockade. Since Armenia received most of its petroleum from Azerbaijan and Turkey, the blockade was the first real advantage for Azerbaijan in the war for the Nagorno-Karabakh region.

ANOTHER PRESIDENT

Elchibey remained in power for only one year of his five-year term. He fled Baku in 1993 to a self-imposed exile in Nakhichevan, claiming that he left to avoid civil war from breaking out. Heydar Aliyev, former first secretary of the Communist Party in Soviet-ruled Azerbaijan, seized power and gained control of the government in Baku. He was installed as parliamentary chairman on June 15, 1993, explaining that because of Elchibey's "inexplicable and unwarranted absence," he had assumed "the duties and responsibilities of the presidency of Azerbaijan."

On June 30, Aliyev named Colonel Guseinov to head the new government. In August, a public referendum ousted Elchibey, and on October 3 Aliyev was elected president with 98.8 percent of the vote.

Following another power struggle, Aliyev dismissed Guseinov as prime minister on October 6, 1994, and chose Faud Kuliyev to fill the spot. He stressed that he, Aliyev, was head of the government and described the outgoing cabinet as "a den of criminals." He vowed to file

WHO COMES NEXT?

Azerbaijani president Heydar Aliyev is a dynamic, politically savvy leader. Many experts feel he is one of the few qualified leaders for Azerbaijan and are concerned that his health is failing.

Evidence of Aliyev's own concern about his health began with an August 24, 2002, referendum that offered more than 40 constitutional amendments. The most controversial of the amendments called for a change in the presidential succession process. It would call for the prime minister to replace the parliament speaker as the first in line to succeed the president in case of incapacitating illness, death, or resignation. Political observers suggest that Aliyev might appoint his son as prime minister and then resign.

The referendums were approved by more than 96 percent of the voters, with 88 percent of eligible voters casting ballots, according to Azerbaijan's Central Election Commission. However, the Office for Democratic Institutions and Human Rights, an international organization, criticized Azerbaijani authorities for not providing enough time for public debate of the constitutional changes.

In February 2003, Aliyev, who has diabetes, came to the United States for prostate surgery. He also used the visit to help gain U.S. president George W. Bush's support for his reelection bid later in the year.

charges of treason against Guseinov, who had fled to Russia. (Guseinov was extradited to Azerbaijan in 1996 and was sentenced to life imprisonment in early 1999, following his conviction on more than 40 charges.)

Yet another crisis erupted in March 1995, when rebel interior ministry forces led by Deputy Interior Minister Ravshan Javadov staged an attempted coup. It was put down but many people died, including Javadov. President Aliyev accused Russia of plotting to destabilize his government in concert with hard-line exiles, specifically Mutalibov.

After nearly four years under a modified Soviet-era constitution, Azerbaijan adopted a new basic law in November 1995. The new government is a federal multiparty republic with a unicameral legislature. The constitution calls for a strong presidency. People are elected to a national assembly in two ways. One hundred are elected from single-member constituencies, and 25 from party lists based on how many votes the party received.

Executive power is vested in a head of state who is popularly elected for a five-year term and who appoints the prime minister and other cabinet members. The president acts as the head of state, while the prime minister performs duties similar to those of the Senate and House majority leaders in the United States.

The legislative balloting in November 1995 and February 1996 further entrenched Aliyev's regime. There was no pretense of a free press or freedom of speech. The courts, which traditionally had bowed to the country's leader, handed down a series of harsh sentences, including the death penalty, for opposition activists convicted of subversion. Russia also gave its stamp of approval to Aliyev in April 1996, when it arrested both ex-president Mutalibov and former defense minister Rakhim Gaziyev in Moscow. Gaziyev was extradited to Baku, where he had been sentenced to death by a military court just two months earlier. Mutalibov escaped extradition on a legal ruling by the Russian procurator general.

Kuliyev's actions as prime minister came under increasing criticism from both the people and Aliyev, most notably for the slow pace of economic reform and the privatization of industry and farming. On July 19, 1995, Aliyev announced that he had accepted Kuliyev's resignation "on health grounds." He also announced that he had dismissed several economic ministers and state managers. The following day, Artur Rasizade was appointed prime minister and Nadir Nasibov became chairman of the State Privatization Committee.

Aliyev was reelected to a five-year term in October 1998. The New Azerbaijan Party, which is aligned with Aliyev, won a majority of seats in the elections. However, many prominent politicians and opposition parties boycotted the election because they felt the government had too much control over the balloting process. The United Nations and OSCE observers reported serious electoral violations, including limits on freedom of the press and the refusal to allow opposition parties to voice concerns or run for election.

The cabinet resigned on October 20, as constitutionally required, and Aliyev reappointed Prime Minister Artur Rasizade on October 23. Many other incumbents were subsequently returned to the cabinet, although Aliyev took several months to make the appointments. At the same time, Aliyev sought to gain a closer relationship with Russia, Armenia's closest ally in the controversy over Nagorno-Karabakh, by offering Russia greater control over Caspian-basin natural resources.

New elections on October 15, 2003, created a sense of déjà vu in Azerbaijan. Once again organizations such as Human Rights Watch cited the current government's record of manipulating election procedures, repressing political opposition, and even condoning violence against the opposition. Despite these concerns, though, Aliyev was reelected and recognized by the European Union and the United States.

The Economy

Azerbaijan's economy is highly dependent on its vast reserves of oil and natural gas near and in the Caspian Sea. This has been the case throughout most of the 20th century and likely will continue to be the case well into the 21st century. The country also has great potential as an agricultural exporter due to its extensive fertile lands and variety of climate zones.

The United States imposed Section 907 of the U.S. Freedom Support Act at a time when Azerbaijani forces held the upper hand in Karabakh. This prevents direct U.S. aid being given to the Azerbaijani government until the U.S. president decides that Azerbaijan is "taking demonstrable action to cease all blockades and other offensive uses of force against Armenia and Nagorno-Karabakh." The U.S. government adopted the sanctions against Azerbaijan after coming under strong pressure from Armenian-American groups. This hampered Azerbaijani recovery efforts to some extent, while many Azerbaijani people feel that this is unfair considering that some 15 percent of Azerbaijan's territory has been under Armenian occupation since 1994.

The U.S. government suspended article 907 restrictions in the aftermath of the September 11, 2001, terrorist attacks, although it still gives less money to Azerbaijan than to its sister countries.

Before the collapse of the Soviet Union in 1991, Azerbaijan supplied oil to the Soviet Union, although that had dwindled considerably during the 1980s, when oil was discovered in Siberia. It also had exported agricultural crops such as cotton and fruit to the Soviet republics.

In the years immediately following the breakup, the country was more consumed with the war with Armenia over Nagorno-Karabakh than with building the economy. As a result, inflation reached 1,500

An Azerbaijani woman carries a box on her head in downtown Baku. Most of the country's citizens live in poverty and must scrounge clothing, food, and items to sell on the streets. (AP Photo/Sergei Grits)

percent by 1994. It also saw a great influx of refugees from the Nagorno-Karabakh region as well as from Armenia and Georgia. Since the cease-fire with Armenia, the economy has improved somewhat. Growth in gross domestic product was 6.1 percent for 2002 and more than 8 percent for 1998.

Despite these seemingly healthy trends, huge economic problems remain. Unemployment is high, with nearly eight job seekers for every vacancy, and only one in 14 unemployed persons is officially considered unemployed. As a result, most do not receive jobless benefits. Nearly half the citizens live below the poverty level.

Wages also are very low. The average weekly wage in Azerbaijan in 1999 was only $10, but even the country's highest-paid people are poorly paid by international standards. Azerbaijani citizens working for a major Western oil company earn on average less than $1,000 a month.

THE OIL INDUSTRY

As one of the oldest oil exporters, Azerbaijan's government understands the wealth lying just beyond its shores. However, it is less savvy about the political implications of this natural resource.

For example, in 1997 President Aliyev signed a $7.5 billion contract between the state oil company and a consortium of 10 foreign oil and gas reserves led by British Petroleum. Azerbaijan had granted an increased stake in the venture to Turkey, which angered Iran. Russia, however, had an even stronger reaction. It rejected its legitimacy, arguing that the Caspian Sea was the joint possession of five countries (Azerbaijan, Iran, Kazakhstan, Russia, and Turkmenistan) and that each should share in its exploitation.

WHO OWNS THE CASPIAN SEA?

While much of Azerbaijan's economic future hinges on its ability to export its large supplies of oil and natural gas, efforts to get at those reserves have been stalled again and again over territorial disputes with other countries on the Caspian Sea. An April 23, 2002, summit meeting with the presidents of the five countries surrounding the Caspian Sea was ineffectual, leaving the borders legally undefined.

While negotiations continue, Iran has claimed an area that would fall under Azerbaijan's rights if the area were divided by coast line. In the summer of 2001, for example, an Iranian gunboat threatened ships carrying out survey work for BP Amoco (working for Azerbaijan) in an area of the sea claimed by both Iran and Azerbaijan. In June 2002, Iran announced its decision to develop Caspian resources lying along the Azerbaijani shore.

Russia, in turn, supports Azerbaijan's interests, even though Russia and Iran have no territorial disputes in the Caspian. The reason is that Russia is set to profit from Azerbaijan's oil fields. In addition, the threat of conflict perpetuated by Iran has hampered investment in Russia's sector of the Caspian. To show its support following Iran's June 2002 announcement, Russia's president, Vladimir Putin, called for massive military exercises in the Caspian Sea and a general buildup of forces in the area.

The U.S. government had to intervene to help negotiate an agreement. The consortium agreed that two pipelines from the Caspian Sea would be used, one an upgrade of the existing pipeline running through Russian territory to the Black Sea and the other through Georgia and potentially to Turkey. The Iranians were excluded from the consortium, which angered them. However, Azerbaijan allocated the Iranians a 10 percent stake in the next phase of Caspian oil development.

This situation could have been avoided if Azerbaijan had been more prepared to take over its own oil industry. However, the years immediately following the breakup of the Soviet Union left the country without the funding or the educated labor force to take advantage of its vast oil reserves. Oil money that could have stayed in the country if Azerbaijan had been equipped to take over the oil industry itself is now being sent to companies in the United States, Great Britain, and elsewhere.

The country does reap many benefits from these partnerships, however. Most important, its labor force is learning to run the machinery necessary for oil production. Under the Soviet government, Russian and Armenian technicians were sent in to man the machinery,

An Exxon oil worker in Azerbaijani waters represents the economic future for the country as it works to build alliances with oil companies around the world. (Courtesy ExxonMobil)

depriving Azerbaijan of the "human capital" it would need to gain self sufficiency in the oil industry.

Azerbaijan has a large economic stake in the oil being mined by the various consortiums. Azerbaijan receives a share of the profits. Likewise, oil pipelines are built across the country, which are then taxed accordingly. As a result, the production and export of crude oil accounts for nearly 60 percent of the country's economy today.

The much-touted Baku-Tbilisi-Ceyhan pipeline, which began construction in September 2002, could boost Azerbaijan's economy if it lives up to its promises. However, the project has hit snags at every stage, from planning to construction, and political events such as the U.S.-Iraqi war have delayed construction. The longer the project takes to complete, the

THE BAKU-TBILISI-CEYHAN PIPELINE

Slated to run through Azerbaijan, Georgia, and Turkey, the Baku-Tbilisi-Ceyhan pipeline is considered the economic hope of all three countries. Construction began on September 18, 2002, for the 1,000-mile pipeline estimated to cost as much as $2.9 billion. The pipeline is projected to have a capacity of about 50 million metric tons of oil per year.

Proponents, including the United States, say the pipeline is a potential force for stabilization in the region because it would provide a reliable and substantial source of revenue that is largely independent of Russian influence. It also would create necessary jobs during both the construction phase and after.

However, not everyone is enthusiastic about the project. Russia initially opposed the pipeline in large part because it circumvents Russia and gives the United States greater influence in the area. Some engineers also consider construction of the pipeline to be a daunting task over the mountainous terrain. Others claim the area does not have enough oil to achieve an economic payoff.

Yet another concern is the general state of corruption and lawlessness in Georgia. Even the pipeline's proponents are concerned about the necessity of paying bribes to Georgian contractors and suppliers. Others are concerned that the many groups in Georgia loyal to Russia—such as greater the danger that the Russian oil-pipeline network will meet the energy needs of countries that otherwise would turn to the BTC pipeline.

AGRICULTURE

Azerbaijan has solid potential as a future exporter of agricultural products. Before the breakup of the Soviet Union, it was a major supplier of cotton, fruit, and caviar to other Soviet republics.

Agriculture produced 19 percent of the country's gross domestic product in 2000 and employed about 38 percent of the workforce. Cotton is the leading cash crop, followed by wine, grapes, fruit, vegetables, and tobacco. Wheat and barley are the principal grains harvested. Mountain

people in Abkhazia and South Ossetia, as well as some people in the military—may openly sabotage the project with terrorist acts.

The groundbreaking ceremony for the construction of the Baku-Ceyhan oil pipeline, which begins in Sangachal, Azerbaijan, was met with hope and concern. It promises jobs and greater wealth from oil exports, but many are concerned that corruption and terrorism will derail the line. (Courtesy BP)

pastures are used for sheep grazing. Tea, citrus fruits, and olives are grown in the subtropical Lankaran Lowland in the southeast. The coastal regions also produce both fish and caviar, while the mountainous regions are large producers of lumbers.

Since the breakup of the Soviet Union, the country has had to deal with other concerns than getting its agricultural economy more export-oriented, though. The war with Armenia over Nagorno-Karabakh consumed more than 33 percent of the country's budget in 1992 through 1995. As a result, there was little money left to help educate farmers used to a Soviet system of collective farming on how to deal with a free-market economy. This has led to an imbalance in the type of products brought to market and, in some cases, to foodstuffs rotting in trucks because they were not in demand.

At the same time, the country has to deal with other problems in its agricultural industry. The land is polluted from years of overusing pesticides and fertilizers. The country's packaging equipment is unsuited to today's rigid export standards, and its transportation system is marred by frequent blockades and stoppages as a result of the dispute with Armenia over the Nagorno-Karabakh region.

OTHER INDUSTRY

A privatization program was introduced in September 1996, and within three years more than 21,000 small enterprises had passed into private hands. Many of these were farms and extremely small enterprises such as retail operations, restaurants and one- or two-worker shops.

Azerbaijan's other industries have lagged behind the other Caucasus republics in terms of privatizations, in large part because the leaders took several years to turn their attentions away from the fight with Armenia and onto the domestic crisis.

Nearly all the industry in Azerbaijan is associated very closely with the oil industry. This includes oil refining, the manufacture of petroleum-related equipment, and chemical processing. Azerbaijan also produces iron ore, aluminum, copper, and zinc, as well as industrial minerals such as iodine and bromine, precious and semi-precious gems, and marble. These products accounted for about 21 percent of the exports in 2002.

Other industrial products are associated with the country's large agricultural output. These include silk, cotton textiles, carpets, and wine. They accounted for almost 11 percent of the country's exports in 2002.

NEEDED INFRASTRUCTURE

It is natural to assume that Azerbaijan will continue to look to its oil industry and agriculture as the combined backbones of its economy in the years to come. However, if it is to build a strong economy, it first must deal with an aging, ill-equipped infrastructure system.

The Caspian Sea is a natural waterway linking Azerbaijan with Russia, Central Asia, and Iran. However, the country's major ports, in Baku, are under-equipped to handle much more water traffic than they currently are receiving. Azerbaijan also has very few of its own mariners willing to ferry goods to other countries. Until the country has more of its own boats equipped to haul agricultural products and industrial goods other than oil, it likely will not make large gains in its economy.

Likewise, products must be transferred to Baku before they can be loaded onto ships heading for Russia and Asia.

While railroad lines more than doubled in the Soviet period to nearly 1,300 miles today, the railroads do not cover enough of the country to make it practical to transfer goods from remote regions to Baku. At the same time, these rail lines now have gone more than a decade without repair or upgrading.

Rail lines leaving the country also need significant improvements if they are to handle more traffic. Few rail lines exist going into neighboring Iran, Russia, Georgia, and Armenia. The ones that do are old and in need of repair. Those going into Armenia are still under blockade.

During the Soviet era, a rail line extending north was the country's principal route for transporting goods. Regional disputes have since occasionally closed the railroad. Azerbaijan now depends on a railroad through Georgia to ports on the Black Sea for much of its imports.

The country has about 17,000 miles of paved road, mostly extending along the Caspian Sea north to Russia and South to Iran. Other paved roads connect Baku with Tbilisi in Georgia. This represents the beginning of a truck transportation industry that could handle some of the internal transport of goods, especially food items from the lowlands to the populated cities on the coast. However, the economy has prevented many trucking lines from developing. In addition, trucking is not a feasible method of transporting goods across mountains because it is both time-consuming and more dangerous than rail transport.

People in the outlying regions of the country still must deal with dirt roads. When these were kept up, under the Soviet system, they were a reliable method of transportation. Today, however, many of the mountain roads are crumbling away and those in wetter climates are nearly impassable during rainy seasons.

As it works to build a stronger transportation system, Azerbaijan also must get other aspects of its infrastructure up to date. The country's system for generating electricity suffers from lack of money for repairs and new investment. In 1999, some 86 percent of the electricity came from thermal plants fueled with by-products of the country's refineries and natural gas. These inefficient plants were not capable of supplying enough electricity to power existing industry, much less an expanding industrial base.

As a result of these infrastructure concerns, the republics of the former Soviet Union are Azerbaijan's main trading partners. Russia, Ukraine, and Turkmenistan purchase the bulk of exports as well as supply most imported goods. Azerbaijan has been developing trade relations with Iraq, Turkey, and the United Kingdom but likely will not be able to extend its reach much further until it has the transportation systems in place to handle long-range exports.

Religion and Culture

The Azerbaijani culture is a fascinating mixture of European and Middle Eastern cultures. While more than 90 percent of the country's citizens are Muslim, the Soviet era saw a large influx of European influences that have been stepped up since independence.

Unlike its sister Caucasian countries, Azerbaijan did not have a significant intelligentsia class before the breakup of the Soviet Union. The emergence of this group has had a major influence on the current development of the arts and other cultural aspects of Azerbaijani life. As a result, there is a sharp difference between modern Azerbaijani culture and the traditional culture of just a few years ago.

A newly constructed mosque fights for attention with the oil towers on Baku's skyline. (AP Photo/Efrem Lukatsky)

RELIGION

Islam was introduced in the area of present-day Azerbaijan during the seventh century, and Shi'ite Islam was established as the official religion of the Azerbaijani people in the 16th century.

During the Soviet period, religious leaders were persecuted, mosques were closed or destroyed, and religious practice was officially condemned. Many of the people fell away from the traditional practices of their religion, including the veiling of women and prayers said throughout the day.

Since independence, the religion is gaining support again. Nearly everyone in the country says they are Muslim. However, they do not practice the religion with the fervor of their Iranian counterparts. Most women do not wear the traditional clothing and the prayers are said more when convenient than on a strict regimen.

About 70 percent of the Muslims practice Shi'ite Islam, and about 30 percent are Sunnis. Although that distinction would be important in most other predominantly Muslim cultures, it is not a crucial distinction in Azerbaijan. The groups live and work side by side.

There is some concern that there will be a rise in Islamic radical activity. Azerbaijan has expressed concern about the war in Chechnya, located on the northeast border of Georgia, and the potential it has to spread radical Islamic beliefs in the Caucasus. Azerbaijani officials also have accused Iran of trying to promote radical Islamic beliefs among Azerbaijani people. There also have been small outbursts of radical Islamic activity, possibly fueled by the country's poor economic conditions.

The country also has a small but strong current of Zoroastrian beliefs left over from its pre-Islamic days. Practiced mostly in the countryside, these people believe that there is only one god, Ahura Mazda, the Lord of Wisdom. They are best known for their temples, which contain naturally occurring fire due to the oil rising from the earth.

CULTURE

Azerbaijan had little unique culture until about the 11th century. Before that, prose, poetry, and oral history recitations called *dastans* were influenced by Zoroastrian works and other pre-Islamic texts. Even after the Azerbaijani people began to see themselves as unique, Persian and later

Turkish influence remained a staple of Azerbaijani culture. Not until the influx of oil workers in the 1800s did Azerbaijan's authors, musicians, and artists begin to create truly unique works.

Ancient epics, such as the *Dada Qorqut* from the 12th century, which chronicles the struggle for freedom among the Azeri people, and authors, such as Nizami Gancavi from the 14th century whose most famous work, *The Story of Layla and Majnun,* narrates the story of two lovers who must overcome tradition and the objections of their families to find their destiny, are part of the literary heritage. Fuzuli (1494–1556) wrote poetry and prose in Turkish, most notably the poem *Laila and Majnun,* the satire *A Book of Complaints,* and the treatise *To the Heights of Conviction.* His works influenced dramatic and operatic productions into the early 20th century. Schoolchildren still read Fuzuli's works in their original Turkish dialects, which are very similar to modern Azerbaijani.

Traditional Azerbaijani art used Persian and Islamic styles and techniques. It included pottery, ceramics, metalwork, carpet making, calligraphy, and manuscript illumination. Azerbaijani decorative arts were marked by especially exquisite craftsmanship and rich ornamentation. To this day, Azerbaijan is famous for its carpet-making. Azerbaijani carpets are known for their bright colors and intricate patterns.

The ancient Azerbaijani musical tradition has been kept alive by musicians known as *ashugs,* who improvise songs while playing a stringed instrument. Another early musical form was the *mugam,* a composition of alternating vocal and instrumental segments. Among the 90 minutes of world music sent into outer space with the *Voyager* spacecraft in 1977 are 140 seconds of Azerbaijani *mugam.*

The unusual architectural heritage of Azerbaijan also reflects the country's multilayered history. There are many artifacts from the prehistoric past, but the Islamic period left its most distinctive imprint on Azerbaijani architecture. Mosques, palaces, mausoleums, inns, and fortresses all carry the rounded style of Islamic architecture, as well as the rich blend of colors and mosaic pictures on the walls, although today most of these are drab and in need of cleaning. Perhaps the most interesting piece of architecture is the 12th-century maiden Tower, a landmark of Baku (and a principal feature of the James Bond movie *The World Is Not*

Enough). Legend has it that a distraught medieval maiden flung herself from the top of the oval-shaped rampart.

The modern literary tradition emerged in Azerbaijan after the completion of the Russian conquest in the 1800s. The writings are marked by their concern for spreading the ideas of enlightenment, rationalism, and education. This concern led to the formation of a separate literary language based on spoken Azerbaijani. This new language gradually replaced Persian.

In the early 1900s, literature received a powerful boost. Seen as the "Age of Three Revolutions," referencing the Russian revolution of 1905, the Constitutional Revolution of 1905–07 in Persia, and the Young Turk revolution of 1908–09 in Turkey, the writers of this time attempted to represent the hopes and concerns of young Azerbaijanis who were increasingly disquieted by the war in their lives.

Perhaps due to the country's Islamic tradition the fine arts never became popular in Azerbaijan. Although the country has its share of paintings, sculptures, and other fine arts, none of these artists are seen as either distinctly Azerbaijani or as exceptionally accomplished on a worldwide level. Instead, the country seemed to intensify and focus its artistic endeavors on the written and spoken word during the 19th and 20th centuries. After 1945, a new literary tradition began to emerge. Called the "literature of longing," this dealt with the theme of unity between Russia, Iran, and Azerbaijan.

Azerbaijan shares the world passion for soccer, although its team is not up to world-class standards. Wrestling is a popular pastime, in large part because of the country's Turkish roots. The country claimed a silver medal in wrestling in the 1996 Olympics and has a two-time world champion in women's sumo wrestling.

Another popular pastime is playing board games. Chess is very popular—world champion Garry Kasparov was born in Baku—as well as *nard*, a board game similar to backgammon.

Daily Life

Daily life in Azerbaijan is not significantly different from that in other former Russian republics. Day after day is filled with the basic necessities of living. Work can be hard to find, so when money does come into the

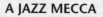

A JAZZ MECCA

Jazz came to Baku along with the oil industry in the early 1900s and continued to gain in popularity. Most of the world's best jazz musicians and composers spent at least some time in Baku, whether as a stop on a world tour or on a private pilgrimage to find out what this part of the world could give to their art.

During the first decades of the Soviet regime, jazz was outlawed. In fact, any type of music played on the saxophone was outlawed. The saxophone solo in "The Bolero" was played by a bassoon in the Soviet republics during this time.

This did not stop jazz from developing, though. Vaqif Mustafazade (1940–79), a pianist, created a fusion of American jazz and traditional Azerbaijani improvisational music called "mugam jazz." His music used improvised rhythms and scales with moody Muslim-style vocals based on traditional Azerbaijani *meykhana,* a rhythmic poetry similar to contemporary rap.

With the death of Stalin, the prohibition on jazz gradually loosened and Mustafazade became internationally known. He won international jazz festivals and was applauded by the likes of Dizzy Gillespe and B. B. King.

Mustafazade died suddenly at the age of 39, but his daughter Aziza (1969–   ) continues the tradition of mugam jazz. She has released several CDs and has a large following in Europe.

household, it usually is spent on necessities. During leisure time, the family members enjoy simple pleasures such as sporting events, good cooking, and talking with friends and family.

LIFE IN THE CITY

Many Baku men are employed in oil-related sectors. Some may spend weeks away from home. Either way, the work is physically demanding. Although some Azerbaijani have been moved into white-collar positions such as technicians, most still work the blue-collar jobs while the foreign oil companies bring in their own engineers and other experts.

Many also are unemployed. If this is the case, the father of the family likely spends many hours at a local teahouse, talking to friends about which companies are looking for workers and what he must do to get a job. He likely takes on daily jobs just to bring in some money. He might drive a taxi for a day, help out at an oil-processing plant, or work as a day laborer at a farm outside the city.

The mother will take care of the small household; most city-dwelling families are small because housing is difficult to find and unemployment is high. The family probably lives in a Soviet-era apartment that looks just like thousands of other apartments in the city. The elevator is likely in need of repair so, if the family lives on a top floor, mother will haul laundry and groceries up several flights of stairs.

WHAT GRANDMA LIKES TO COOK

Food is a very important part of life in Azerbaijan and, because the country has ample farmland, it is relatively inexpensive. Grandmother will start the day's main evening meal with a plate of aromatic green leaves and bread. She may serve yogurt or cheese, and a cucumber and tomato salad. The main dish will probably contain fish or lamb. The meat is often skewered and grilled as a kebab then served with a sour-plum sauce or a sweet cucumber and onion sauce. If she has obtained chicken, she may make *lavengi,* a casserole of chicken stuffed with walnuts and herbs.

For lunch, grandmother will again prepare bread and salad, but this meal will have soup instead of a main dish. *Dovga,* a thick soup with yogurt, rice, spinach, and fennel, is a favorite. Another favorite is *Dusbara,* small lamb-stuffed dumplings served in a meat broth. She probably made *qutab* the night before so it could be sent with father for lunch. This dish is a type of pancake turnover stuffed with minced lamb, cheese, or spinach.

Grandmother will spend a great deal of her day making an elaborate dessert, especially if friends or other family members are visiting. *Baklava* and *halva* are typical desserts. Both feature chopped nuts sandwiched between thin layers of dough. For special events, she also will make *pesmak* for the children. These tube-shaped candies are made from rice, flour, and sugar.

Grandmother and grandfather probably live with the family as a way to save money because their pension checks are small, if they get them at all. Grandfather will head out around midday to meet friends in the local park, where he will smoke cigarettes, play chess, and generally criticize the government's handling of the economy and the fight with Armenia over Nagorno-Karabakh. If asked, he will pick up some fresh bread or green vegetables on the way home in the afternoon.

Grandmother will help with the housework and will baby-sit any children while mother runs errands, such as picking up the day's groceries or searching the various markets for silk and cotton fabric that she can sew into clothing. Grandmother also will do much of the cooking, relying on a menu of meals that she grew up with.

Keeping up the household is not an easy venture for mother. Because the city water is undrinkable, all water must be boiled. The family probably does not have hot water for bathing, so baths happen only occasionally and then the water must be heated on the stove first. Electricity is sporadic, so mother must make sure that any activities requiring electricity, such as sewing, are kept up to date.

The refrigerator probably runs on natural gas so that it will stay running when the electricity is shut off. There are no luxury appliances, such as microwave ovens.

Because the family is Muslim, they celebrate many of the Islamic holy days, including Gourban Bayram. This Festival of Sacrifice commemorates Abraham's test of faith when God ordered him to sacrifice his son Isaac. People visit family and friends during the five-day festival and the head of the household slaughters a sheep, which is used as the central meat for the upcoming feast. Since Azerbaijani people often are not practicing Muslims, they may use this time to visit family and friends and hold large feasts, although they likely will serve dishes made of store-bought mutton.

The next festival is Novruz Bayram. This New Year festival is rooted in Zoroastrian tradition and marks the return of spring. It is a time for parties, picnics, and family reunions. Children receive presents at this time, and both mother and grandmother will do spring house cleaning.

Asura is a Shi'ite holy day that commemorates the martyrdom of Imam Hussein, grandson of the Prophet Muhammad, at the battle of Karbala in A.D. 680. Men will parade through the streets dressed in black, hitting themselves with metal flails while virtually every community holds a passion play that reenacts Hussein's murder. Father probably does not participate in this, although the family may venture to see one of the passion plays.

During the holy month of Ramadan, devout Muslims refrain from eating, drinking, and smoking during daylight hours. It ends with a three-day festival of eating and drinking. Most Azerbaijani people are not devout Muslims, so they do not fast through the entire month. Some will cut back by eating smaller meals and not smoking or drinking alcohol.

Whether the family actively participates in these events or not, they will be aware of them and observe their neighbors' rights to participate in them. They will be respectful of the fact that restaurants and markets may be closed during daylight hours during Ramadan, for example.

The children in the cities attend school from the time they are five years old until they are about 18 years old. At that point, the boys must serve in the army for two years. Most of the young men will be used to back up the peacekeeping forces in Nagorno-Karabakh but will never actually be sent to the region.

The schools still run on the Soviet model, so boys and girls attend classes together. They learn math, science, history, social studies, the Azerbaijani language, and Russian. After school, boys and girls alike may participate in a chess club, a wrestling team, or a soccer team. Children who do not do exceptionally well in school will be routed to technical schools by the time they are about 13. Here they will learn a trade, such as working on oil rigs or at oil-processing plants.

The children who pass their preliminary exams will work hard at school and on homework so that they pass their exams when they are 17 and 18. If they pass with high marks in four or more subjects, the boys may forego the army to attend college, although they will later be expected to serve the army in their professions. The girls can go directly to college or technical schools, although, because of the Muslim tradition, many will simply work at retail or secretarial jobs until they marry and start families.

The family cannot afford to attend the opera or ballet when it comes to town, but the adults do make excursions to local clubs to hear American-style jazz as well as Azerbaijani music. Traveling musicians also frequently play in the park for free.

Although they live in poverty, children still find time to play in Baku. (AP Photo/ Misha Japaridze)

LIFE IN THE COUNTRY

Life in the country can seem very different from that in the city. The family almost certainly lives on a farm. Because most of the farms were bought back from the government when the privatization program began, the family may own anywhere from 10 to 100 acres of land that it manages itself. It also may have bought a larger farm by joining with other family members.

The house is small but larger than the city apartments. As in the city, grandmother and grandfather likely live with the family. Unmarried aunts and uncles also likely live in the household to help with the house and family chores before they go on to start their own lives.

Living on a farm means constant work for everyone, including the children. Mother may be responsible for small animals such as chickens, while father tends the beef cattle or sheep. If the family raises fruits and vegetables, father tends to the plants while mother and grandmother keep a large kitchen garden near the house.

Farming communities maintain the Soviet style, where households surround a small market area. The fields then radiate from that central area. The children have just a short distance to walk to school, and mother or grandmother has just a short distance to go to purchase essentials. Father will go into the market area perhaps once a week to visit with his friends and discuss buying a new plow or a large tractor as a community.

Grandmother may never leave the house. She will care for the young children, tend the garden, cook meals, clean house, and generally back up mother for all the work that must be done.

Mother is very frustrated when she goes to the market because there are very few goods available in the stores. The old distribution methods have broken down, so even basic items such as cloth are difficult to obtain.

Meals in the countryside are not as elaborate as those in the city, and they often are much larger. Instead of intricately spiced sauces, the lamb will be simply cooked over an open flame. Desserts will almost always be simple fruit that is in season in the family's garden.

After they get home from school and do their farming chores—such as feeding the young lambs—the children may gather with nearby friends for a quick soccer match or game of chess.

The people in the country probably have some electricity but it may be just one simple outlet that works only a few hours a day. It might be located on a large pole outside the house, so long extension cords will be attached to a single light. They may have a battery-operated radio to receive news and to listen to music, but it will be used for only an hour or so each night so the batteries do not wear out quickly.

Whether living in the city or the country, the people of Azerbaijan are anxious for change. They watch the government closely and read newspapers whenever they have a chance. They are looking toward a more affluent future and have little patience left for a government that is not taking them in that direction. As a result, all the adults are likely to talk politics often and may even go to political meetings in the evenings.

Cities

The cities in Azerbaijan are similar to those in other former Soviet republics. They have developed largely based on the need of a system that no longer exists. As a result, they are working to restructure themselves into working communities that meet the needs of an independent country.

At the same time, Azerbaijan offers a great deal of variety in its cities and towns. Coastal cities quickly give way to charming country villages. Desolate desert towns exist mere miles from picturesque mountain villages.

BAKU

Baku, the capital of Azerbaijan, is the largest city in the Caucasus. With 1.7 million people, it was the fifth-largest city in the entire Soviet Union. On paper, it is the most prosperous of the Caucasian capitals, although most of the prosperity is a result of foreign investment. The actual Azerbaijani citizens do not see much of the money unless they happen to work in the service industries, such as running a restaurant that caters to foreigners.

The origin of the city's name is disputed. Some claim it comes from the Persian *bad kube,* which means "city of winds." Others claim it is derived from an ancient word meaning "sun" or "god" because it was connected with Zoroastrian religious rituals.

There is evidence that people lived in the area during prehistoric times, but the first mention of it as a true city appears in the ninth century A.D. It flourished as a port and trading center in the Middle Ages, in large part because it has one of the best natural harbors on the Caspian Sea.

OIL AND BAKU

Oil was scooped from shallow holes in Baku as early as the 10th century, when it was used to light lamps. In 1872, the oil boom arrived and Baku's population jumped enormously overnight. The oil barons built large mansions, and the downtown became a beautiful tree-lined boulevard flanked by expensive shops selling the world's goods.

In the 1930s, the search for oil moved into the waters along Baku's coast. By the end of the decade, the Caspian Sea around Baku was littered with offshore platforms, derricks, and wells. Pipelines seemed to sprout from everywhere.

Today the city is extremely polluted from the unscrupulous oil industry that began in the late 19th century and lasted into the middle of the 20th century. The city was literally used only for its access to oil some 60 miles from its shores in the Caspian Sea. The workers and the governments taking the oil did not waste time on making sure they were environmentally responsible or that they were creating a beautiful place to live. They looked for the cheapest, easiest methods they could to obtain the oil.

This large Exxon oil-drilling rig represents new ventures between Azerbaijan and major oil companies. (Courtesy ExxonMobil)

SURAXANI

Suraxani lies about eight miles northeast of Baku and is famous for its Zoroastrian fire temple. The *atesgah* (temple) is built on the site of a natural gas vent that was sacred to this ancient religion as early as the sixth century.

The gas flame in Suraxani is now fueled by the town's gas mains because the natural gas cannot support a flame any longer, a result of drilling that reduced the gas pressure. However, Yanar Dag is a complete hillside of scorched earth covered in flames about a half mile long and up to three feet high. It lies just a few miles north of Baku.

GENCE

With 294,000 people, Gence, also called Gandzha, is Azerbaijan's second-largest city. Straight west of Baku, it is the last settlement of any size before reaching the Armenian border.

Gence was founded in the fifth century A.D. and was once an important center for Azerbaijan. It is an industrial city that supports much of Azerbaijan's non-oil-related industry. At the western end of the country's lush farmland, the city has many cotton textile mills that ship goods into Georgia and beyond.

Gence also is important because it lies so close to Nagorno-Karabakh. It served as a staging area for armed conflicts and continues to be a military town for peacekeeping soldiers on leave.

SEKI

Although Azerbaijan is not known as a tourist destination, Seki is one of the few towns that has relied on the tourist trade for many decades. It was the site of the Soviet "tourist trail" in the Caucasus countries and still maintains much of that flavor. With 63,000 people, it sits near the northern border with Russia, just slightly west of midway from Baku to the western border of the country. The country's history has mostly been lost, but archaeologists have discovered evidence of people living in the area more than 2,500 years ago.

In the 18th and 19th centuries, the town flourished as a staging post and resting place on the route from Baku to Tbilisi and Turkey as well as into Russia. At that time, there were five working "caravanserais," companies that supplied and led caravans. The town also was known for its silk weaving and embroidery during this time.

QUBA

With 27,000 people, Quba is the main town of northern Azerbaijan. It was founded in the 18th century when the local khan moved his capital there from Xudat farther to the east. It serves as a trade center for people living in the mountains near there and hosts some tourists from Baku on weekends. Its only distinguishing feature is the post-Soviet-era Bet Knesset Synagogue, a sign that this town is the center of Azerbaijan's small Jewish population. It is known for its Turkish carpets but does not produce enough of them for it to be considered an industry.

ZAQATALA

Zaqatala has 26,000 people. It sits in a thickly forested area of the Caucasus Mountains. Because of this, it is one of the country's most popular tourist destinations. The town has little industry and serves as a center for farmers and people living in the mountains to visit.

The town has one interesting historical note. Its fortress was used as a prison for the sailors from the Russian battleship *Potemkin,* whose mutiny at Odessa in 1905 is often seen as the early beginnings of the Russian Revolution of 1917. Until recently, the town had a large statue of one of the Potemkin mutineers' leaders overlooking the town.

NAGORNO-KARABAKH

Nagorno-Karabakh, an autonomous republic under the Soviet Union, is located in the southwest corner of the country. The largest town, Stepanakert, sits centrally in the region and was built during the Soviet period. It is largely industrial, with just a few shops and one museum. Its population continues to fall from the Soviet-era high of about 10,000 people to fewer than 5,000 today, largely a result of people moving to Armenia and Azerbaijan.

Just a bit north of Stepanakert is Gandazar, a very small town. Its only significance is a monastery that claims to have the skull of St. John the

Baptist. Although not officially part of Armenia, the residents of the Nagorno-Karabakh region consider themselves culturally part of the Armenian nation, in large part because more than 90 percent of its inhabitants are Armenian. It has just one main road traveling from south to north through the enclave.

NAKHICHEVAN CITY

Nakhichevan is technically an exclave of Azerbaijan, a portion of the country that is entirely surrounded by foreign territory. It has borders with Armenia and Iran, as well as a small four-mile border with Turkey. Nakhichevan City has about 67,000 people and sits about midway along the length of the border it shares with Iran. Although it is about as far as possible from Armenia, even at this farthest point, the Armenian border is less than 20 miles away.

Legend claims that it was settled by Noah himself after his ark settled onto Mount Ararat in what is now Turkey. Whether true or not, it has flourished as a trading center from as early as 1500 B.C.

Because of the tense relations with Armenia, Nakhichevan remains a very isolated city. It maintains some trade by transferring goods to and from Turkey via its small shared border. It also sends and receives goods to Iran and to the larger portion of Azerbaijan via Iran.

For the most part, however, the small region is relatively self-sustaining by living off of local farmland and some imports. Nakhichevan City serves as the central meeting place and trade area simply because it is centrally located in the region.

NOTES

p. 77 "He was installed as parliamentary chairman . . ." *The Statesman's Yearbook* (London: Palgrave Macmillan, 2002), p. 65.

p. 78 "He stressed that he, Aliyev, was head of the government . . ." *The Statesman's Yearbook* (London: Palgrave Macmillan, 2002), p. 65.

p. 80 "The United States imposed Section 907 of the U.S. Freedom Support Act . . ." Armenian Assembly of America Fact Sheet. *Section 907 of the Freedom Support Act.* Released April 12, 2002.

p. 82 "While negotiations continue, Iran has claimed . . ." McConnell, Artie. "Iran Announces Unilateral Decision To Develop Caspian Resources," June 4, 2002. www.eurasianet.org/departments/business/articles/eav060402.shtml. Downloaded May 4, 2003.

p. 86 "Azerbaijan also produces iron ore, aluminum, copper, and zinc . . ." Azerbaijan Altpedia Online. file://A:\Azerbaijan-AtlapediaOnline.htm. Downloaded July 16, 2002.

p. 87 "While railroad lines more than doubled in the Soviet period . . ." Virtual Azerbaijan. http://scf.usc.edu~baguirov/azeri/azerbaijan4.htm. Downloaded March 3, 2003.

7

GEORGIA

The Land and Its People

Georgia is a land of great contrasts. At 27,000 square miles, just slightly larger than the state of Virginia, it contains three very different climate zones and a wide variety of typography, including everything from frigid mountain regions with more than 700 glaciers to subtropical zones so lush that it is considered one of the most beautiful vacation spots in Eastern Europe.

The country is bounded by Russia in the north, Turkey in the south-west, Armenia in the southeast, Azerbaijan in the east, and the Black Sea on the west. It is separated from Russia by the Greater Caucasus mountain chain, with the highest point being Mount Shkhara at more than 17,000 feet. Slightly farther to the south and west, bordering Turkey, the Lesser Caucasian mountain range rises to points below 15,000 feet but still offers a rugged, Alpine climate. Another mountain range, the Likhi, divides the country almost in half down the middle. The country has six mountains over 15,000 feet and 10 more that are over 12,000 feet. More than half the land in Georgia lies higher than 1,000 feet above sea level.

The mountain ranges, along with the Black Sea, serve to divide the country into its various climate regions. A humid subtropical climate dominates in the western part of the country near the Black Sea. Here, temperatures are very moderate, reaching slightly below freezing in the winter months and reaching into the high 70s Fahrenheit during

August, the hottest month. This northwestern region bordering on Russia, called Abkhazia, was once the most popular resort area in the Soviet Union but since 1991 has suffered due to civil strife.

The mountain Alpine climate is very cold, with highs of just 50–60 degrees Fahrenheit in July and August, and lows well below zero for as long as five months in the winter.

To the east of the Likhi mountain range, the country is much hotter and drier. Annual precipitation is 50–110 inches and temperatures can reach into the 90s. This area has more plateaus and flat lands.

The country has heavy snowfall in the mountains, but the melt does not produce lakes. The largest, lake Paravani, is just 14.4 square miles. Lake Kartsakhi is 10 square miles. The country also is dominated by just one main river, the Kura, which starts in Turkey and flows east through the capital, Tbilisi, and then through Azerbaijan to the Caspian Sea. In total, it travels nearly 850 miles. In western Georgia, the Rioni and Inguri Rivers flow from the mountains to the Black Sea. Several other rivers, all shorter than 500 miles long, flow north into Russia and eventually to the Caspian Sea.

There is little in terms of freshwater lakes and rivers in any part of the country, but Georgia has much water lying below the surface. The country has more than 2,000 mineral springs capable of producing more than 130 million litres of water a day.

Georgia also has a great deal of limestone, which has washed out into areas to produce a large network of caves across the country. The Pantiukhin cave is more than 5,000 feet deep.

Because it has high mountains, a subtropical coastline and near-desert terrain, the vegetation of Georgia is extremely rich and diverse. It contains nearly every type of habitat found in Europe, as well as several found in Asia.

There are more than 100 different species of animals in Georgia. There are more than 300 types of birds, more than 50 different reptile species, about a dozen amphibian species, more than 150 different types of fish, and several thousand different types of small sea animals such as mollusks. Even more important than the variety, however, is the fact that the country is home to more than 60 different animal species that are considered rare, threatened, or endangered.

THE PEOPLE

Georgia has 5 million people, about the same as the state of Washington. About 70 percent of them are ethnic Georgians. There are more than 100 different ethnic groups, including large groups of Armenians, Russians, Azerbaijani, Abkhaz, Ossets, and Ajarians.

The official language of the country is Georgian, a language unrelated to any other major world language. The language belongs to the South Caucasian, or Kartvelian, language family and uses a distinct alphabet that was developed in the fifth century A.D. Georgian remained the official language of the republic during the Soviet period, although Russian predominated in communications from the central government in Moscow. Most of the country's ethnic minorities do not speak Georgian; some do not even speak Russian.

The large city of Batumi and several smaller towns line the Black Sea coast, shown here. (Courtesy Library of Congress)

WHERE THEY LIVE

The largest cities are very predictable to find—just look for water. Tbilisi, the capital city, is located to the east of the Likhi mountains. It has more than 1.2 million people and lies in the Kura River Valley. Kutaisi, the next largest city, is across the mountains to the west. It has 240,000 people and lies at the junction of the Enguri and Rioni Rivers. Batumi, with 136,000 people, lies on the Black Sea coast in the southern half of the country within just a few miles of several smaller coastal towns.

About 60 percent of the population—and nearly all ethnic Georgians—live in towns and cities. One-third of the people living in towns and cities live in Tbilisi.

Virtually every citizen can read and write at least one language, even if it is not the official language of the country. More than half of the population has finished secondary school, and about 15 percent of the population has gone on to school beyond high school. In fact, during the time of Soviet rule, the country boasted the highest average level of education in the Soviet Union. It also had the highest number of medical doctors.

The biggest factor affecting the Georgian population today is aging. Since 1991, people have not been able to afford large families, so there are not as many young people being born as there are people reaching retirement age. About 13 percent of the population is over 65, but that number is expected to rise into the middle of the century. That fact, in turn, will put more pressure on the remaining citizens to supply social services and goods for the aging population.

The Government

Georgia gained its independence from the USSR on April 9, 1991, but it was not an easy transition. The next few years were especially bloody and contentious, as rival political and religious groups tried to establish dominance and two regions demanded independence.

In May 1991, Zviad Gamsakhurdia was elected Georgia's first president of the post-Soviet era. He was ousted in early 1992 after a number of opposition parties charged him with "imposing an authoritarian style of leadership." Gamsakhurdia responded by arresting the opposition leaders and declaring martial law in Tbilisi. National guards and other paramilitary forces besieged his headquarters, forcing Gamsakhurdia to flee to Chechnya, from where his followers staged several unsuccessful attempts to reinstate him by force.

A Military Council took power until tensions eased. Former Soviet official Eduard Shevardnadze was chosen in October 1992 to lead the country as acting chairperson of the State Council, the country's interim legislature, and Shevardnadze was elected to the post by popular vote later that year.

This time of violence held Georgia back on the international scene. The United States and the European Union did not recognize the country until the end of 1991, and the country was not admitted to the United Nations until July 1992.

In August 1995, Georgia adopted a new constitution that reestablished the presidency. The constitution defines Georgia as a democratic state with freedom of speech, thought, conscience, and faith guaranteed.

The president is elected to a maximum of two five-year terms. He is authorized to appoint a council of ministers that report to him. The constitution also established a new unicameral legislature consisting of 235 members, who are elected to four-year terms. Of its members, 85

Georgian president Eduard Shevardnadze won more than 70 percent of the vote when he was elected in 1995 in one of the fairest elections in any former Soviet republic. (Courtesy NATO)

are elected by simple majority in single-member districts and 150 are elected on a proportional basis, with the number of delegates from each party corresponding to the proportion of the total vote that party receives.

As Shevardnadze was en route to sign the new constitution approved five days earlier, his car was bombed. He escaped with minor injuries, and the security minister was named as one of the three instigators in the bombing. Shevardnadze survived two other assassination attempts after this as well.

In November 1995, presidential and legislative elections took place, with recognition around the world that they were among the fairest and freest elections to date in any former Soviet republic. Shevardnadze was overwhelmingly elected as president, winning more than 70 percent of the vote. His party, the Citizens' Union of Georgia, won the largest number of seats in the new legislature. While the remaining seats were won

---

ETHNIC REGIONS IN TURMOIL

Abkhazia and South Ossetia have caused problems for Georgia since the early days of the Soviet Union's breakup.

In July 1992, the leaders of Muslim Abkhazia declared their republic independent. Georgian authorities sent troops into Abkhazia, and heavy fighting broke out in the region. By October 1993, Abkhazian forces, with covert assistance by Russia, had expelled the Georgian militia, and more than 200,000 ethnic Georgians had fled the region.

A U.S.-sponsored agreement was reached in April 1994 that established some peace for the Abkhazia region. Under the agreement, Abkhazia was to remain part of Georgia while maintaining a high degree of autonomy. A force of 2,500 Russian peacekeeping troops would guarantee that fighting did not break out again, although guerilla activity continues to occur.

Violent fighting between Ossets and Georgians living in the region began in 1989, when the majority of the population in South Ossetia demanded unification with North Ossetia, within the Russian Federation. Georgia's parliament subsequently abolished South Ossetia's autonomous status in late 1990 and declared a state of emergency in the South Ossetian capital, Tskhinvali.

by members of many different parties, most of the individuals were considered sympathetic to Shevardnadze's views.

Despite the relative homogeneity of political views in the country, Georgia fell into a state of nearly complete dysfunction under Shevardnadze's leadership. In fact, some observers in South Ossetia say a major block to the peace process in the region is the huge money being made by smuggling goods into and out of Georgia through South Ossetia. Many observers call it a "failed state," a region with no legal controls.

The region that raises the greatest concern is the Pankisi Gorge, which lies just east of South Ossetia on the border with Russia's troubled Chechnya region. Russia claims that the area is being used by Chechen rebels and Islamic radicals as a safe haven as they conduct guerilla warfare in neighboring Chechnya. The Georgian government has been unable to bring the region fully under control.

Another referendum called for integration with the Russian Federation, and in April 1992 Georgian troops attacked Tskhinvali. More than 400 Georgians and more than 1,000 Ossetians were killed before a cease-fire was declared in June 1992.

The region has been relatively stable with just minor squabbles and power plays: South Ossetia held elections in 1999 that Georgia declared illegal and subsequently cut the electricity supply to South Ossetia to just 30 minutes a day. South Ossetia's budget has been entirely financed by Moscow, and North Ossetia has backed off on its idea to unify the two regions. Economic contacts between South Ossetia and Georgia have been strengthening.

However, in his October 11, 2002, state-of-the-nation address, Shevardnadze said Georgia strives to restore Tbilisi's authority over both Abkhazia and Ossetia while refraining from threatening action.

A third region, Ajaria, achieved a significant degree of autonomy from Tbilisi under its leader, Aslan Abashidze, who ruled the region between 1991 and 2004. The government in Tbilisi accused Ajaria of failing to pass on significant amounts of tax and customs duties. In late 2003, a state of emergency was declared in Ajaria after Abashidze refused to recognize the full authority of Saakashvili as president of Georgia. The standoff ended in May 2004, when Abashidze resigned and left the region, and Saakashvili imposed direct presidential rule on the area.

In September 2002, Russian president Putin attempted to test his country's power over Georgia by citing a United Nation's statute concerning the right of self-defense as a reason to send soldiers into Georgia in order to protect Russia's borders from Chechen insurgents.

Shevardnadze responded by arresting a number of exiled Chechens and extraditing a suspect in the 1999 bombings of Moscow apartment blocks. However, the region is considered essentially lawless to this day, and Russia continues to question Georgia's commitment to containing the Chechen separatists.

In the meantime, the United States has stepped up its relations with the country. Following Putin's threat to send military into the Pankisi Gorge region, the United States said it would not sanction such an operation. The United States also proposed a trilateral security arrangement in which the United States and Russia jointly tackle Georgian instability. Citing a possible "domino effect"—if the Russians sought military control over a former Soviet republic, it might go on to do the same in other countries—U.S. military advisers said the United States should have a "strict and sharp" response to any Russian military action in the Pankisi region.

In late 2001, the United States also agreed to send military advisers to Georgia to help train the country's army, an event that further solidified the relationship between Georgia and the United States. The volunteer effort received lukewarm response from Georgia's military despite being touted as important by top Georgian politicians; this is likely because top Georgian military leaders were Russian-trained and felt allegiance to their origins. Many older, Soviet-trained officers resigned in a public display of protest.

In general, crime and corruption are the key issues in Georgia today. On June 18, 2002, Peter Shaw, a British businessman working as a consultant for the European Union, was the first of several European businesspeople and government workers to be kidnapped. Several police officers allegedly witnessed the abduction but did nothing to stop it. He was released in early November 2002, but Georgia's leaders claimed he was committing criminal acts. The European Union adamantly denied that Shaw was doing anything illegal.

This first kidnapping was the cornerstone event the European Union needed to withdraw or delay much of its economic aid to Georgia. In addition, by early 2003, both the World Bank and the International Monetary Fund, raised the possibility of cutting off operations in Georgia. Both groups said that corruption was the major problem and that the need to pay bribes

In elections held on January 4, 2004, Mikhail Saakashvili was elected president. (AP Photo/ Alexander Zemlianichenko)

to get business done was increasing dramatically.

Georgia's citizens looked toward the coming elections in early November 2003 as a chance for change. Opinion polls showed that Shevardnadze's supporters would lose their majority in parliament, paving the way for new tactics to improve the country's economy. Shortly before the election Shevardnadze promised to hold democratic and fair parliamentary elections.

However, when election day came, Shevardnadze either did not or could not keep his word. International observers said "the elections were marred by spectacular irregularities." Immediately, people began protesting in the streets, demanding for Shevardnadze's resignation and a new election.

The government waited for more than two weeks to announce its election results, finally saying that two parties who supported Shevardnadze had again gained control of parliament. This announcement stimulated even more protest. The streets in Tbilisi filled with people yelling for new elections.

The protest finally ended on November 23 when, after meeting with opposition leaders and Russian foreign minister Igor Ivanov, Shevardnadze announced his resignation. In elections held on January 4, 2004, Mikhail Saakashvili was elected president. The parliament confirmed his presidency on March 28, 2004.

It is no surprise that many countries, including the United States, supported Saakashvili's party, the United National Movement, as it attempted this political turnover. Although Saakashvili is seen as relatively inexperienced, many of his party's ideas support more progressive economic and crime-prevention programs. As a result, Georgian citizens and world leaders alike lauded what is now called the Rose Revolution as a major step in helping the country overcome its problems.

As a sign of new times, parliament has since adopted the flag used by Saakashvili's party during the Rose Revolution. Previously the flag of a medieval Georgian kingdom, the five-cross banner had not been used for 500 years.

The Economy

Georgia's economy is as varied as its geography. In fact, most of the economy is a direct result of the terrain. Mountains, valleys, and the Black Sea provide direct economic opportunities, while the climate that exists because of these surface features provides even more opportunity.

The mountains provide the major industry for Georgia. They have pushed up out of the earth large deposits of coal, oil, peat, iron, copper, zinc, mercury, and other minerals, making small mines a major industry in the country. At the same time, nearly 40 percent of the mountainous land is forested, resulting in a large export industry of wood products. The valleys and plains between the mountain ranges offer very fertile land for farmers to produce citrus fruits, grapes, tea, tobacco, and vegetables. Abundant rivers flowing from the mountains provide water for crop irrigation while the lush pastureland also means livestock can be inexpensively produced.

The country's unique location in the world also makes Georgia a key player in international trade and tourism. The Black Sea coastline provides one of the most beautiful vacation spots in Europe while also supporting a large shipping industry. At the same time, the country serves as an overland trade route for petroleum traveling from Azerbaijan's and Iran's rich reserves to ports on the Black Sea. The best rail transportation routes across the Caucasus Mountains travel through the middle of Georgia.

Unfortunately, the traumatic domestic events following independence have created a nearly complete economic collapse with inflation of more than 1,500 percent. The country's gross domestic product declined by 60 percent between 1990 and 1995 the greatest amount of any former Soviet republic. Georgia became increasingly dependent upon foreign financial and humanitarian aid during this time.

Energy shortages also contributed to the economic downfall. The government rationed both electricity and heating fuel throughout the early 1990s. Power outages also were frequent as the country struggled to provide enough power with its hydroelectric plants because it could not afford to run the oil-burning plants. As a result, many industries were closed.

As the politicians were busy dealing with internal unrest, they also could not spend the much-needed time to reorient Georgia's economy to make best use of its resources. During the Soviet period, it was a major supplier of electric locomotives and jet fighters, items that are not especially well-suited to the raw materials available in the country nor to the long treks across the mountains or the Black Sea to make deliveries of the products. Agricultural production was oriented to tea, citrus fruit, grapes, mineral water, and wine, which were exported to other Soviet Union republics. This left Georgia needing to import grain and meat, although its land was perfectly suited to raise these products.

ECONOMIC PROGRESS

The economy has stayed stagnant into the first decade of the 21st century. It has received both money and advice from the International Monetary Fund (IMF) as well as individual countries such as the United States. It still has a large trade deficit and debts of more than $1.7 billion. In 2002, both the IMF and the World Bank, however, expressed frustration with Georgia's high rate of crime and corruption and said they were considering suspending operations in Georgia.

In September 1995, the Georgian government introduced a new currency, the lari, in an attempt to stabilize the economy. Inflation has since slowed to about 7 percent, and the country has maintained modest growth for both industrial and agricultural production every year since 1995. However, these numbers are misleading in terms of the situation for the average citizen. Unemployment is rampant, and more than half the population lives below the poverty level.

Georgia's gross domestic product in 2002 was $15 billion. Agriculture, including forestry and fishing, contributed 32 percent of the total. Industry, including manufacturing, mining, and construction, produced 13 percent of goods. Services, which include trade and financial activities, accounted for 55 percent of the gross domestic product.

The government adopted a policy of converting the state-owned businesses to private ownership shortly after independence but saw little success during the turbulent first half of the 1990s. By 1997, however, more than 90 percent of retail operations were private. By mid-1998, more than 90 percent of all small businesses had been privatized and 80 percent of larger businesses were privately owned. The electrical-supply industry was privatized in 1998. However, the country is having a difficult time finding buyers for its telecommunications industry.

Economic growth and reform slowed in 1998 and remains lower than 1997 levels due to a severe financial crisis in Russia, drought, and political events, including a major outbreak of hostilities in Abkhazia and an assassination attempt against the president. However, the period also saw completion of the country's first major infrastructure project since independence, a pipeline that carries oil from Baku, Azerbaijan, to Supsa, on Georgia's Black Sea coast. Foreign tankers transport the oil to Turkey and Europe. In September 2002, construction also began on the Baku-Tbilisi-Ceyhan pipeline (see sidebar, page 84). The pipeline could be a step in the right direction for Georgia's economy, but state corruption and concerns about potential sabotage continue to slow down the process.

AGRICULTURE

Agriculture provides nearly half of all employment in Georgia. Not only does the country produce food, it also processes foodstuffs and trades them with other countries. Although agricultural production fell by nearly half from 1990 to 1995, help from foreign governments in terms of both money and advice has brought it back up to the 1990 level.

Key to the agricultural economy today is its breadth. Georgia has one of the most diverse agricultural sectors of any of the former Soviet republics. The country's agricultural producers are beginning to convert much of their land from the former Soviet system of one-crop management to more diverse crops that offer greater economic opportunities. The lowlands of the west have a subtropical climate and produce tea and citrus fruits. Fruits such as apples and grapes grow in the uplands. Georgia also produces large amounts of vegetables and grains because of its long growing season.

Livestock agriculture also is important. Milk cows and goats graze on the ample pasture land in the valleys, producing enough milk to make cheese a major export item in the country. Sheep and beef cattle graze on the scrubbier highlands leading into the mountains, providing an inexpensive protein source for the nation's people, as well as some export business.

With more than one-third of the land in Georgia containing forests, the lumber industry is a natural component of the economy. Most of the lumber stays within the country to be used as private heating fuel and building materials.

Because agricultural production is nearly year-round in much of the country, the processing of agricultural goods is the most significant part of Georgia's industrial activity. Canning plants, cereal-production facilities, and cheese-making plants have seen strong growth. Georgia's agricultural exports are citrus fruits, tea, grapes, canned foods, cigarettes, mineral water, and wine. In the more arid regions of the country, cotton is produced. Some is exported as rough cotton, but it more often is used to produce textiles and footwear. Wine and mineral water were major exports during Soviet times, and the country is working to build that business again.

MINING

The three mountain chains criss-crossing Georgia's landscape may make it difficult to travel in the country, but they also provide a great deal of opportunity for mining. Georgia has abundant depots of manganese, iron ore, molybdenum, and gold as well as coal and some petroleum. Marble, alabaster, and shale also are mined.

Although mining declined significantly in the early 1990s as a result of the internal tensions and expensive fuel prices, it has grown more than 75 percent from its 1995 low. The country counts coal, copper, iron, steel, and manganese among its main exports.

INDUSTRY

The industrial sector provides just 10 percent of Georgia's employment. During the Soviet era, several manufacturing operations produced military goods, including fighter jets and clothing. While the airplane-production industry has dried up, many of the skilled workers it produced have turned to manufacturing precision tools and trucks. These are now major export items for Georgia. Likewise, the military-clothing industries have converted to consumer clothing. Cotton fabric, clothing, and footwear also are leading exports for Georgia.

Still, the industrial sector has been the slowest to recover since independence. It continues to produce at less than 25 percent of its Soviet-era capacity. Factories that have not been used or updated for more than a decade are now physically crumbling throughout Tbilisi.

TOURISM

The Georgian Black Sea coast was one of the favorite vacation spots for Soviet citizens. After the breakup of the Soviet Union, though, tensions in Georgia curtailed the tourism industry. It is unlikely to rebound until the hostilities are well under control.

TRADING PARTNERS

When it was under Soviet rule, Georgia was required to export most of its goods to other Soviet republics. Today Turkey is its principal partner,

The Pankisi Gorge is considered one of the most lawless areas in the world today. Georgian troops must patrol the area constantly. (AP Photo/Shakh Aivazov)

accounting for more than a quarter of total trade. Other leading purchasers of Georgia's exports are Russia, Armenia, Azerbaijan, Turkmenistan, and Ukraine.

THE FUTURE

Georgia has several problems it must overcome before it makes a complete economic recovery. First, it must find a way to rebuild its crumbling infrastructure. Because no buyers have yet been found for the transportation or telecommunications industries, they remain state-owned. And the state simply does not have the money to put into repairing systems that have not seen improvements in at least 15 years. Yet without those improvements, goods cannot flow, and trade with other nations becomes difficult.

A burgeoning refugee population also is straining the country's resources. Renewed fighting in neighboring Chechnya, Russia, has generated concerns that the conflict will spill over into Georgia. In the meantime, several thousand Chechen refugees moved into Georgia's Pankisi Gorge in late 1999. Likewise, more than 150,000 native Georgians have moved out of Abkhazia.

Yet another concern is the loss of the country's intellectual elite. A slow-growing economy combined with increased violence has caused many well-educated people to leave the country for other parts of the world. This deprives Georgia of the minds it needs to continue its reformation.

Corruption also is a major problem. Georgia is known for being difficult to do business with despite laws designed to encourage foreign investment. Officials at all levels frequently ask for bribes for the most basic services. Poor-quality work is accepted as long as the bribe is big enough, and contracts are frequently given to the company or individual supplying the most under-the-table money. Corruption is so pervasive in the culture that it has undermined the credibility of the government and its reforms while preventing many foreign countries from entering Georgia to set up business.

Another issue directly relating to corruption is the state's failure to collect taxes. Customs officials, police officers, and nearly every group that has the opportunity to benefit from corruption uses it as a way to gain a better standard of living. For example, businesses frequently pay more than $100 a month in bribes just to avoid paying taxes. In addition, the Abkhazian government refuses to transfer its share of taxes to the central government. As a result, the country collects less than one-third the tax dollars it should.

Religion and Culture

Georgia has a very rich culture that derives from the ancient religions practiced in the country, as well as the country's unique geographic location between Europe and Asia. Despite centuries of foreign domination, Georgia has been able to preserve a unique cultural tradition that combines all the diverse elements of its population.

To view Georgia's dance and art, to hear its music, and to read its literature is to be transported to a world that is part Asia, part Europe, part Christian, part Muslim, and somehow complete Georgian. The culture evokes a sense of spirituality with the mountains through ancient traditions while adding the dimension of constant change brought about by centuries of conquest and foreign travelers.

RELIGION

The Georgian identity has been closely tied to religion since the introduction of Christianity in the early fourth century. As a result, about 60 percent of all Georgians are Christians of the Georgian or Armenian Orthodox Churches (normally called the Armenian Church). About 11 percent of the population is Muslim, although these are divided among three major groups and several smaller groups. The country has had a Jewish population for more than 2,500 years, as well as a small population that follows the ancient Yezid religion. There also are small groups of Catholics and Protestant faiths.

Christians and Muslims rarely interact. Most small towns and villages contain people practicing only one religion. In Tbilisi, the capital, a large part of the city is devoted to Muslim homes, businesses, and places of worship and serves as a city within a city.

The Georgian Orthodox Church is very conservative. It uses an early translation of the Bible, predating the King James version by several hundred years. Today's Georgian monks and priests are still very fundamentalist. They regard Catholicism and Protestant religions as dangerously liberal and maintain that there are no other legitimate churches.

Members practice their faith using religious icons, statues, and other symbols both at home and in the churches. Their ancient churches and monasteries are elaborately decorated with murals, frescoes, and statues. Even the ancient tombs are decorated with stonework and engravings. Georgian cemeteries are often small and devoted to just one family. However, they can be very intricately designed, sometimes including buildings and benches. Easter celebrations frequently occur at graveside.

Culturally, the Muslim communities fit in well with the Orthodox churches. Although their beliefs are different, both religions are conservative.

During the Soviet period, religious practice was strongly discouraged. Although religious leaders in some countries were persecuted and the churches closed, the Georgian Orthodox Church was allowed to function openly. No one is sure why the Soviet Union let this occur when officials were so adamant that other religions could not function.

CULTURE
Architecture

Georgia's ancient culture is evident in the country's architecture, which is renowned for the role it played in the development of the Byzantine

This Mugan church in the settlement of Petropavlovskoe shows distinctive elements of both Georgian and Byzantine architecture. (Courtesy Library of Congress)

style. The earliest churches date to the fourth century and combine the style of Byzantine basilicas with Georgian traditions. Instead of long, rectangular structures, the Georgian churches emphasized the central area. They were usually circular with a cupola for a roof, possibly mimicking the design of eastern-Georgian homes from the same time period. The homes were built with a central roof that tapered to an open point used as a chimney.

In the 17th and 18th centuries, palaces were built with a definite oriental influence, representing Persian domination. The Russian annexation of Georgia in the 19th century brought a more European influence to the architecture. The 20th century is primarily devoted to functional, boxlike Soviet architecture, although the Georgians tended to decorate their buildings with elaborate, often eclectic metalwork.

Literature and Art

Georgia had a "Golden Age" of cultural development in the 12th and 13th centuries. It produced a great deal of artistic and literary work, much of it unique. This may be because, unlike its sister countries, the lush countryside and warm climate near the Black Sea resort area provided an easy living and ample time for contemplation.

Georgia's art and literature were relatively stagnant from this time until the early 1900s when many talented students were able to study in Paris or other Western European cities. Elena Akhvlediani (1898–1975), a romantic painter, was named a People's Artist of Georgia in 1960 for her

THE KNIGHT IN THE PANTHER SKIN

Georgia is the only country in the world known to have a "National Epic," a poem that serves much as a national anthem in other countries. Shota Rustaveli's long poem, *The Knight in the Panther Skin* describes three heroes' quests and includes testaments to the fact that love and friendship can overcome evil.

Supposedly, Rustaveli was Queen Tamar's treasurer late in the Golden Age. Many of the poem's philosophical musings have become proverbs in Georgia. Even during Communist rule, the main street of the Georgian capital was named after Rustaveli.

varied works that often portrayed traditional rural life. She also gained fame as a book illustrator and theater and film designer.

Georgia's greatest contribution to the art scene from 1500 through today is actually more often seen outside Georgia. Many of the 20th century artists' works are in Paris or Moscow museums. At the same time, many European artists have spent extended vacations in Georgia gaining inspiration from the beautiful countryside.

Sculpture

Icons depicting Christ, the Virgin Mary, and the saints were produced on wood or etched into silver then covered with gilt during the Golden Age. Sculpture most often took the form of elaborate frescoes on the outside of churches. (Although frescoes often are associated with paintings, they are actually colored plaster that, when used in thick layers, becomes sculptural.) Elaborate mosaics also decorated many churches, although few survive today.

The tradition of sculpture continues today. Elaborate metalwork graces even the most simple structures, and several extremely large sculptures produced in the 1960s and 1970s depict Russian heroes and folktales. In the 20th century, several Georgian sculptors have gained international recognition. Among them is Elguja Amasukheli, whose monuments are landmarks in Tbilisi.

Folk Music

Georgian folk music is known around the world for its complex, three-part harmonies. Men and women sing in separate ensembles with entirely different repertoires, although women's songs and singing ensembles are relatively rare.

To those trained in Western music, Georgian music often sounds off-key and disharmonious. It often has as many as eight different voices all improvising and taking turns singing solos. Most Georgian folk songs are peculiar to individual regions of Georgia, with distinct differences in melodies. The inspiration is most often the church, work in the fields, or special occasions.

Musical instruments were not as common in Georgian history as vocal music, but they have existed for at least 3,000 years. Both reed (such as the clarinet, oboe, and bagpipe) and stringed (such as the guitar, lute, and ukulele) instruments are found in Georgia, although they bear only passing resemblance to traditional European instruments.

Popular music maintains the simplistic style of its ancestry. Devoted to common themes such as love and romance, the simple poetic lyrics often are accompanied by basic guitar music.

Like the music, Georgian dance has developed into very segregated and regionalistic styles. The Georgian State Dance Company, founded in the 1940s, is renowned around the world for its renditions of Georgian folk dances in which the men wear brightly colored costumes and dance on their toes.

Most Georgian dances began as pagan rituals. For example, men will perform hunting dances or soldiers' dances. Another dance has men using swords to fight over a woman. These dances are often specific to regions of the country and are performed in bars or at festivals to show loyalty to the region.

Film and Theater

Several movies from the 1970s and 1980s satirized Soviet life, but the single most important film of the Soviet era was Tengiz Abuladze's *Repentance*. This work won international acclaim when released in 1987. It showed the consequences of Stalin's Great Terror of the 1930s by depicting the reign of a fictional local dictator.

Georgians also excel in theater, claiming more acting companies than any other country its size among the former Soviet republics. The Tbilisi-based Rustaveli Theater has been acclaimed internationally for its stagings of works by William Shakespeare and German dramatist Bertolt Brecht.

Sports

As with any European country, Georgians are fanatical about soccer. They have their own league, and most Georgian men follow it religiously. They also enjoy basketball and have a hall devoted exclusively to playing professional basketball. The country also has its own traditional sports, including *tskhenburi,* an event like polo; *chidaoba,* an event like wrestling; and *lelo,* an event like rugby.

Daily Life

Daily life in Georgia is filled with family, friends, and work. Whether a family lives in the country or in the city, they likely live near other family members who visit frequently. They will spend special events together and celebrate both religious and family events with an abundance of food, laughter, and wine.

Because Georgia contains so many different ethnic and religious groups, it is very difficult to say what a typical day is like for any one family. In the Muslim religion, for example, prayers are said several times a day. The Christians also might pray every day, but they do not have rituals as formal as the Muslims do unless it is Sunday or a Holy Day. Christians still often do not attend church services except for special events such as Easter or a wedding.

GEORGIAN CUISINE

Georgian cuisine includes a variety of delicate sauces and sharp spices that are a direct result of the many different traders traversing the country over the millennia. It has influences of both Asian and European cooking while including unique variations based on local ingredients. Many different dishes are usually served with every meal, and no meal is complete without a Georgian beer or wine. Bread with cheese, eggs, and fruit is served for breakfast. Heavier fare is served for lunch, dinner, and snacks.

Georgian foods are very fresh because they usually use only in-season vegetables. They also can be very elaborate, containing grated walnuts, many spices, garlic, and onions. In western Georgia, people use hot chili peppers to season many of their dishes.

Most of the cuisine is based on vegetables. *Lobio,* for example, is simple red or green beans with herbs and spices. *Pkhali* is made with spinach or beetroot paste and includes walnuts, eggplant, mushrooms, and lettuce.

Although there is a large coastline, the cuisine does not include many fish dishes. Lamb and chicken are the most popular meats. These might be spiced with herbs such as tarragon, fruits such as plums, oranges, and tomatoes, or vegetables such as eggplant and carrots. Georgians enjoy putting sauces on their meats. The most common are made from walnuts, plums, or hot chili peppers.

Desserts usually consist of cakes laden with fruit sauces or fresh fruit. They may include cream and nuts as well.

Food can vary greatly depending on location. The diet of people who live high in the mountains likely consists mostly of potatoes and lamb. In the warmer, subtropical regions, people are more likely to eat fruit and vegetables. In the hotter, dryer parts of the country, grain is easier to grow and bread is a staple of the diet.

Music also is something that everyone enjoys no matter where they live or what their ethnic background is. Many men gather once a week or even more often at a local tavern or at someone's house to eat, tell stories, laugh, and sing folk songs. Their wives, meanwhile, will be working in the kitchen to prepare food for the groups.

The children go to school from September to June. If they are in grade school, they only go for about five hours a day. In high school they will go for seven hours. Because the country has many schools, even the children who live on farms are probably close enough to walk.

The parents are very concerned about the education their young children are receiving because it is not as good as the one they received under the Soviet system. The books are often very old and parts of the school are closed down since the country became independent because there is no money for repairs. All sports teams have been canceled because there is no money. The teachers are poorly paid and often unenthusiastic about their jobs.

As the boys in the family reach 18, they will go into the Georgian army for two years, although about 80 percent find the money to bribe a local official.

If they must go into the army, mother will be concerned that they will be sent to one of the old military bases at which some soldiers have gotten radiation burns from old weapons. Mother also is concerned about the treatment of her son in the army. She has heard that the soldiers do not get paid on time, and even when they do receive their pay, it is not very much. Some soldiers have rioted because their housing conditions are so poor.

The family will find many reasons to celebrate, even if they cannot afford to buy expensive food or to travel to visit relatives. On Easter, they will go to visit the family graves and may even have a day-long picnic at the summer house by the graves. If a male friend comes to visit, they likely will have a *supra*, a meal that will last for up to five hours where the men make long, elaborate toasts and drink a lot of wine. If there is a wedding in the family, there will be a huge party that could last as long as three days. There will be a lot of drinking and dancing.

THE SUPRA

Georgians love to have fun. They like to party. They like to sing and dance. They like to make friends. And they like to entertain. These facts combine with the tradition-oriented culture to create an interesting ceremonial dinner with roots that likely extend far back into history, when long-lost friends in the trading business would arrive to tell fabulous stories.

The *supra* is a frequent occurrence in Georgian homes. It is a highly ritualized event that forms a direct line to Georgia's past. It may have begun thousands of years ago as age-old friends returned while traversing their trading routes. Days would be spent swapping stories, eating food, and generally enjoying each other's company before the trader moved on, not to be seen again for several years.

Today the supra will last for an entire evening and well into the early morning. It consists of round upon round of elaborate and long-standardized and improvised toasts, a lot of alcohol, and even more food. As the participants get more and more drunk, the toasts may turn into rowdy songs and dances that promote a man's character and heritage.

The food is made by the women, who stay in the kitchen except when serving or when they are the recipient of one of the many toasts. Like the alcohol, the food keeps coming long into the evening, so that by the time dessert arrives, some guests may be falling asleep at the table.

LIFE IN THE COUNTRYSIDE

Families that live in the countryside are likely farmers. Since independence, the family has likely bought the land they live on and are working hard to make payments on it. In some cases, close friends or family members may have pooled their limited resources to buy the land, so they must make all the decisions as a group.

Life is not easy in the countryside. The people are very poor and would flee to the city if they had the money to move and felt they could find an apartment. The father makes all the decisions regarding the farm, although he also searches out advice from neighbors, experts traveling to the area from other countries, and the grandfather. Today he likely is looking at raising animals, fruits, vegetables, and grains that will make him the most money.

Chances are the father is trying to save money to buy new farm implements, as his old Soviet-style implements are becoming out of date. Although he might prefer a nice new tractor and other equipment of his own, he is likely sharing equipment with other nearby farmers.

Although the farming community is centered around a town, reflecting the Soviet collective agricultural system, father will head into a larger town once every few weeks to bring in foodstuffs that he will trade for money. He might trade some foods directly for items such as radios, televisions, or even a new kitchen stove. Chances are, when the family was much poorer just six to 10 years ago, father had taken the radio and television to town and sold them, so now he is working to replace them.

The mother will spend most of her time taking care of the family. She will clean the house, make the meals, take care of the children, and also help out on the farm. It is likely she has a personal garden that she uses to raise vegetables for the family. She also might have a milk cow or milk goat that she uses for the family's milk. If the family is small, the mother also will do some of the daily farm chores, such as feeding animals or helping plow the fields.

Mother has to plan her day carefully. Water is not always available, nor is electricity. As a result, she fills up water jugs whenever she can. On days when the electricity is running, she will catch up on sewing with the electric machine she has had since she was a little girl.

Once a month, Mother might venture into the nearest city. She probably takes a train. Mother likely has a male escort, such as a brother or brother-in-law. She will be dressed very conservatively. In addition to shopping, she will visit church to say a quick prayer and perhaps light a candle for a deceased relative or a relative that is working in Russia. In this case, she will make sure her head is covered.

Grandmother and grandfather probably live in the same house. If they are in good health, they will help with the household and farmwork. If they are not able to help, mother will see to their needs. If the grandparents do not live with the family, they likely have a very small apartment in a nearby town. Mother would stop by to visit when she went to town.

LIFE IN THE CITY

Life in the city is very difficult for Georgians. Unemployment is very high. Housing is both expensive and poor quality. Social services, such as health care, are nonexistent. Crime and corruption are so bad that the country is nearing what is called a "failed state," meaning that the government has no control over what happens. People must pay bribes for such basic services as water and electricity.

Mother might work part-time at a canning plant or a textile factory. Father might be trained as an engineer or doctor, but he is probably working in a job that pays much less than that. He might be one of the many businessmen trying to start an import-export operation or building a retail store. In this case, he will be very frustrated by the unreliable electricity and the fact that he has to pay bribes to tax collectors and suppliers.

Mother and father probably take the train to their jobs, although there are many options. If their jobs are nearby, they may walk. They also might drive a car. Although gas is expensive, most Georgians own cars and love to drive them.

The schools are the same for children in the country and the city. If mother and father have enough money, however, they have the option to send their children to private schools. In these schools, the teachers are paid more money and the textbooks are up to date. Children who attend these schools almost always go on to attend one of the country's two universities, the University of Tbilisi or Georgian Technical University.

The family probably lives in a very small, rundown apartment. They must plan their days around water and energy shortages. They also may not have heat all day in the winter, so they have to plan to wear heavier clothes. They might wash their clothes in the kitchen sink and hang them on lines around the house to dry.

Grandmother and grandfather might also live in the apartment. The children might sleep on the floor in the living room at night, giving grandma and grandpa the second bedroom. If they do not live with the family, at least one set of grandparents probably lives very close. In this case, the young children might go there after school.

The family lives in a neighborhood of people just like them. All their neighbors will be from the same ethnic and religious groups. They may have many relatives in the same apartment building.

Mother and father worry about all the violence in the past years because they do not want their children to be in danger. They are happy that things seem to have settled down now and are looking forward to working hard to make their life better. Although they like independence,

A typical street scene in Tbilisi, the business and population center of Georgia.
(Facts On File, Inc.)

they may be nostalgic for the Soviet era, when they had good jobs and did not have to worry about feeding the family.

Cities

The towns in Georgia are very small because they must support small agricultural and mining communities. Tbilisi, located in the southeast portion of the country, is the capital. It has about 1.3 million people. Only four other cities—Kutaisi, Rustavi, Batumi, and Sukhumi—have more than 100,000 people. These cities are distributed throughout the regions of the country and serve as gathering places for the many farmers and small industrialists to bring their goods for transport within the country or to other countries.

TBILISI

As the capital of the country, Tbilisi serves as both the business and population center of Georgia. It has an extremely diverse population, a tradition

HOW TBILISI GOT ITS NAME

The most popular legend in Georgia says that the town was founded when the king of Iberia, Vakhtang Gorgasali, was hunting and wounded a deer sometime around the year 450. The deer fell into a hot spring and was healed. Another version of the legend says King Gorgasali was hunting with his falcon. When his falcon caught a pheasant, both fell into a sulphur spring and were cooked. The king feasted on them for lunch.

Tbili means "warm" in Georgian, so the extrapolation becomes obvious. The hot springs that King Gorgasali found still exist throughout the area. There are more than 30 hot springs on the northeastern slopes of Mt. Tabori, which produce about a half-million gallons of water a day.

Still, the truth is probably a bit more mundane. A fourth-century map drawn by the Roman geographer Castorius sited "Tphilado" between Rustavi and Mtskheta, and a bridge was built over the Kura River at the spot of ancient Tbilisi.

Turkish bathhouses in Tbilisi, whose name derives from the hot springs naturally abundant throughout the city. (Facts On File, Inc.)

that goes back to its roots as a trading center more than 2,000 years ago. Many of its residents are not native Georgians. Although the city has fallen on hard times since independence from the Soviet Union, it still offers all the amenities of a big city: cultural activities, shopping, diverse restaurants, and night life.

Tbilisi sits in the valley of the Kura River, which runs through the middle of the city. This provides both a picturesque setting as well as fresh water, hydroelectric power, and transportation. Although the river is not used much for transporting goods to and from the mountains, it served that purpose in earlier centuries.

Tbilisi produces about half of all the country's industrial output. It contains most of the country's factories, although many are not currently being used. It also is a central hub for goods leaving and coming into the country.

KUTAISI

Kutaisi lies about 70 miles west of Tbilisi and was actually a main trading center long before Tbilisi. It was first mentioned in Greek writings from the third century B.C. Some people believe this is where King Aetes, father of Medea, lived.

Whenever the country was divided into eastern and western Georgia, Kutaisi found itself the capital of the west. During the Soviet era, it was the second-largest industrial sector, and its population grew significantly. Now, with industrial production falling throughout the country, the city is very poor and many people have moved to Tbilisi or even out of the country. It has about 240,000 people.

Although there are few cultural centers or historical monuments in Kutaisi, it does have a nice nature preserve just outside of town. One large stone preserves dinosaur footprints from 120 million years ago. There are big underground caves with massive stalactites and stalagmites.

A monastery about five miles from town sits on a wooded hill. It was built as a school in 1106 by King David. Legend is that he wanted to create a second Athens and a second Jerusalem on the site. Many of the former rulers of the country are buried there, and the churches are still standing.

RUSTAVI

During Soviet times, Rustavi was the industrial center of the country. It was established immediately after World War II for just this purpose and hosted a metallurgical plant that was the republic's largest employer. It also had large chemical and pharmaceutical companies. It has a population of 150,000, many of whom are retired or bedridden because of the poor working conditions they suffered at the plants.

BATUMI

Batumi is the capital of the Ajaria region, a semiautonomous republic within Georgia. With 136,000 people, the town has become the new resort area of Georgia. It has the historical distinction of being the place where Joseph Stalin helped instigate a major strike at the Rothschild Oil Refinery. Stalin was exiled to Siberia for this.

Because it lies less than five miles from the Turkish border, Batumi brings in many Turkish tourists. It also is a trade center for goods from and to Turkey and those imported from Turkey. It is the spot where oil from Kazakhstan arrives in Georgia to be distributed throughout the country.

SUKHUMI

Sukhumi is the capital of the Abkhazia region in the far northwest corner of Georgia. Hostilities broke out in the region in the early 1990s because the people felt they should be separate from Georgia. Over the years, most of the Georgians have left, and Sakhumi has become a sort of militaristic ghost town. It is estimated that more than 100,000 of the 250,000 Georgians leaving the area lived in this main city. As a result, whole blocks of housing and industry are empty today.

It is unclear how people make a living in Sukhumi now. Some probably sell goods to the soldiers. The region is known for its excellent farmland, so it is likely that many of Sukhumi's citizens have left to live with friends and relatives in the countryside so they can raise their own food.

Sukhumi used to be a beautiful vacation town on the Black Sea coast. However, the fighting has destroyed some areas of the city, and Russian troops are on patrol constantly. There are landmines in some areas out-side the city, and shooting incidents are still common inside the city.

SAMEGRELO REGION

Although it contains only small towns, the Samegrelo region is very important to Georgia. It is bounded by the Rioni, Tskhenistskali, and Enguri Rivers, the Black Sea, and the Abkhazia and Svaneti regions. On the central-western edge of the country, it has flourished as a region for producing some of the best green tea in the world.

The region has gained importance because it was the home of Zviad Gamsakhurdia, the first leader of Georgia after it declared independence. Although Gamsakhurdia was replaced quickly and had to flee to Chech-nya, many of his followers remain in this region. These people actively oppose the new government.

Because it borders Abkhazia, the Samegrelo region has had to deal with the influx of Georgian refugees fleeing from the fighting in the early part of the 1990s. Many of the people were originally from the area, so they were readily accepted as friends, but the small towns simply did not have the resources to handle the many refugees.

The largest town, Poti, has about 50,000 people. It serves as Georgia's main port on the Black Sea and is likely one of the oldest towns in the country because of this. Small towns along the coastline were popular resort towns during the Soviet era. A marshland area just a few miles from Poti is famous because Hippocrates visited it sometime in the fourth or fifth centuries B.C. He wrote about hot winds, fogs, and people who lived off the boggish land.

Zugidi, the region's capital, is the first town you reach when leaving Abkhazia. It actually has more refugees from Abkhazia (about 72,000) than it has permanent residents (about 52,000). The town was an indus-trial center during the Soviet era but now is struggling to support the refugees. It also serves as a military "leave" town for many of the Russian peacekeeping troops stationed in Abkhazia.

TELAVI

With 28,000 people, Telavi is the largest town in the easternmost part of Georgia known as Kakheti. It serves as a trade center for grape farmers and miners in the area. It also is a small vacation town known as a spot where people start expeditions into the Caucasus Mountains. There are several old churches and a castle in the town. Nearby is an area that held 19 different monasteries, the first built in the sixth century A.D. They are especially interesting because they were built into limestone caves. However, Telavi's biggest claim to fame is the wine produced in the region.

NOTES

p. 108 "He was ousted in early 1992 after a number of opposition parties charged . . ." MSN Learning and Research. http://encarta.msn.com/encyclopedia_761556415_2/Georgia_(country).html. Downloaded November 21, 2002.

p. 112 "Many older, Soviet-trained officers . . ." Areshidze, Irakly. "Pro-Russian Georgian Officers Impede US Military Program," July 29, 2002. www.eurasianet.org/departments/insight/articles/eav072902b.shtml. Downloaded May 3, 2003.

p. 112 "The first kidnapping was . . ." Stier, Ken. "EU Remains Wary of Georgia, Despite Release of Kidnap Victim," November 11, 2002. www.eurasianet.org/departments/insight/articles/eavll2002.shtml. Downloaded May 3, 2003.

p. 120 "The Georgian Orthodox Church is very conservative. . . ." Buford, Tim. *Georgia with Armenia* (Guilford, Ct.: Globe Pequot Press, 2002), p. 45.

8

COMMON PROBLEMS

On the surface it seems as though Georgia, Armenia, and Azerbaijan are wildly disparate nations. They have different ethnic groups, different religions, different cultural traditions, and even different landscapes. They have internal ethnic struggles as well as old animosities between each other, some of which flare up into bloody battles.

However, as the three Caucasus countries of the world, these small countries have a great deal in common, including a difficult transition from Soviet central planning to the free market.

Corruption

Corruption is rampant in all three countries. This is a common problem in societies with high unemployment combined with uncontrolled inflation and deteriorating social services. People find that the only way they can afford to live is if they make money on the side. Police officers may take bribes for not handing out a speeding ticket. People might sell items they received from relatives in Europe.

Unfortunately, in these countries, the corruption has gone far beyond small bribes and a small black-market trade. All three have become world centers for the drug trade entering Europe from Asia. Lax border patrols and import authorities have made it relatively easy for drug cartels to establish operations that are supported with minimal bribes.

Government workers also are corrupt to varying degrees in the Caucasus countries. Police officers may take bribes in almost any country, but the Caucasus countries have seen top administrators skimming monies from foreign-aid packages and tax collections. The result is that some people refuse to pay for services, which, in turn, makes it impossible for the countries to offer those services.

Georgia has developed a council to make recommendations on how to thwart corruption. Unfortunately, it has yet to implement any of the recommended measures, in large part because the corruption runs so deep. Armenia and Azerbaijan simply look the other way and hope that their economies improve along with their policing measures to the point that the typical citizen feels it is not worth the chance to participate in illegal activities.

Crumbling Infrastructure

The very problems that give rise to corruption and crime are getting more and more expensive to fix every day. All three countries have serious problems producing enough electricity because their power plants have not been repaired or updated for more than 10 years. Water cannot be transported reliably throughout Armenia. The transportation systems in the three republics are not just crumbling; they are inadequate to meet the needs of growing economies.

The same is true for the industrial base. Many of the factories in these countries are gigantic Soviet structures that produced all of one type of product needed elsewhere in the Soviet Union. The factories may not have been efficient, but it did not really matter at the time. Now the factories are more than 10 years out of date, and many are so large that they cannot effectively scale back to produce profitable amounts of product.

Both corruption and a crumbling infrastructure hold back badly needed foreign investment. Some countries, such as Georgia, have deteriorated to the point that the International Monetary Fund and the World Bank are unwilling to work with them.

Social Services

Along with basic public utilities, the Caucasus countries also are having a difficult time providing basic public services to their people. In most cases, only about one in 10 unemployed people actually receive unemployment benefits. The elderly often receive less than they must pay for housing and food. Schools and universities are still running, but the teachers are poorly paid, and the best often look for jobs outside the country.

Pollution

The Soviet system also left the countries with severe environmental problems such as pollution. Western Georgia has unsafe radiation levels. Large parts of Azerbaijan's capital city look more like scenes from a post-apocalypse science fiction movie than a 21st century economic center. Armenia and Azerbaijan both have unsafe drinking water in most urbanized areas, while much of the farmland in all three countries has been polluted by the overuse of fertilizer and agricultural chemicals.

The environmental problems also have serious economic repercussions. How is Georgia to rebuild its western resort area when the area is polluted? How will industrial pollution affect health care systems in several decades when the pollutants start increasing cancer rates or produc-

Toxic metallic powders were used at a glass manufacturing facility in Yerevan. The facility is now closed. (Robert Kurkjian)

ing other health issues? How will the farmers be able to grow crops that can be exported to the Western world if they cannot meet the safety codes those countries demand?

As is the case with the crumbling infrastructure, the country must find short-term solutions that allow the use of the systems or land while building toward more pollution-free strategies. To date, that simply has not happened.

Trade in a World Market

Although Armenia, Georgia, and Azerbaijan offer very different natural resources and industrial goods to the world, they all suffer from the same problem. No one in the current government or business world in these countries can remember what it was like to work in a free-market economy. Under Soviet rule, the industrialists produced what they were told and shipped it where they were told. If they made too much or too little and a problem resulted, it did not matter, because they still earned their wages.

This planned economy also created unnatural markets. If the Soviet central planning committee felt it needed more fruit, for example, it would turn land in Georgia that might be better suited to vegetable farming into orchards. The Georgian farmers could not say anything even if they wanted to. Now, however, that land might not produce enough fruit to make it worth the effort. The price to produce it, process it, and ship it would be too high to make it salable. The land should be turned back into vegetable farms, but the farmers only know how to run orchards.

The problems become even more complex when the countries begin dealing with commodities such as oil or other natural minerals. Azerbaijan learned this when it signed a deal with Western oil industries. Russia was very angry and threatened to impose trade sanctions on Azerbaijan if the deal went through. Since Azerbaijan could not survive without Russian imports, it turned to the United States to negotiate a deal that would satisfy Russia.

Foreign Relations

Lest the three countries forget to read their history books, they quickly are learning that trade is what politics are made of. Their countries were built because people wanted to trade goods between Europe, Asia, and the Middle East. Today, as these countries seek aid from Western Europe and the United States, they find they must tread carefully when developing alliances with old trading partners such as Iran.

The problem is amplified by various religious groups and cultural identities. In Azerbaijan, for example, many people feel they are a part of Turkey. They also share a religion with Iran, Iraq, and the rest of the Middle East.

They have inevitably leaned toward the United States, Europe, and former Soviet republics as trading partners, sometimes uncomfortably dissolving "favoritism" agreements with Turkey, for example. But if they become nervous that their new, geographically far-flung allies cannot protect them from incursions by their neighbors, they could develop trade agreements that put them—literally—in the middle of a war between Western cultures and the Middle East.

A New View

As with all the former Soviet republics, the three countries of the Caucasus region have a great deal of catching up to do. They must develop leaders in government and industry that can quickly and reliably guide their countries into the 21st century.

Armenia and Azerbaijan already have had to spend too much time and valuable resources trying to resolve their ethnic conflict in the Nagorno-Karabakh region. Armenia has had other ethnic conflicts that have taken time, money, and lives. Georgia has spent much of its capital on its conflicts in Abkhazia and South Ossetia. Likewise, all three governments have had to deal with infighting, with leaders being ousted or even assassinated.

Without a resolution to end ethnic conflicts, economic recovery will be difficult to achieve. Until the countries in Caucasia begin to view themselves as a single entity with multiple viewpoints, they have little chance of rising out of their current states of poverty.

CHRONOLOGY

200,000 B.C.

Humans first settle the Caucasus region

Eighth century

Area of Azerbaijan is settled by the Medes

Sixth century

Trade is so prevalent in Georgia that tribes organize into governmental groups; area is settled by Greeks and Persians

Third century

Alexander the Great conquers the Caucasus region

190

Prince Artashes creates Greater Armenia

100

Tigranes I enlarges Armenian borders

First century

The Great Silk Road is established; Rome conquers area

69

Tigranes I yields several lands to Rome

A.D. 298

Persian-born Mirian II named king of Georgia as condition of a Roman treaty with Persia

301

Christianity becomes official religion of Armenia

330

Mirian II declares Christianity the state religion of Georgia

600

Muhammad begins preaching

634

Muhammed dies; Muslim armies have conquered Arabian Peninsula

640

Arabs invade Caucasus

300–800

Area changes hands and borders change several times under Persian, Russian, Arab, and Greek rule

885

Armenian prince Ashot takes power of Armenia; Golden Age begins

946

Bagratid dynasty begins rule of Georgia

11th century

Arab rule of Armenia and Azerbaijan

12th century

Georgia reaches its Golden Age under Queen Tamar

1223
Chinggis Khan conquers Caucasus

14th century
Black Death almost decimates Georgian population

15th century
Persia controls Azerbaijan and makes Islam the official religion; Georgian kingdom disintegrates and lands are divided among Bagratid family members; Persia drives Ottomans out of Georgia

1615–16
Shah Abbas solidifies control of Georgia by killing 60,000 people and deporting 100,000

1720s
Ottomans attempt unsuccessful conquest of Georgia; Persia places King Erekle II in control of Kartli kingdom

1747
Nadir Shah, ruler of Persia, is assassinated in palace coup, and Azerbaijani kingdom fragments into khanates

1762
Erekle II unites many regions to create most of modern-day Georgia

late 1700s
Erekle II turns to Russia for protection

1795
Persian forces overrun Tbilisi

1801
Russia deposes Erekle II and annexes the eastern Georgian kingdom; western Azerbaijan annexed to Russian Empire

1803

Construction begins on Georgian Military Highway

1804–13

First Russo-Persian war

1810

Russia annexes western Georgia

early 1820s

Russian Empire gains control of Armenia

1826–28

Second Russo-Persian war

1828

Russia creates border with the Ottoman Empire that finds many Armenians living in the Ottoman Empire

1829–78

Russia absorbs the remainder of Georgia

1880s

Oil discovered off the coast of Azerbaijan; Baku becomes the Russian Empire's fastest growing city

1890

Tensions begin between Turkey and Armenia; the Ottoman Empire destroys all Armenian churches in its lands

1894–96

Turks kill 300,000 Armenians living in the Ottoman Empire

1900

Russia owns 60 percent of Georgian land; most of the merchant class in Georgia is Armenian; intellectuals known as "The Men of the '60s" begin to preach Georgian nationalism; Azerbaijan supplies most of Russia's oil

1905

Beginnings of Russian Revolution create nationalism in Azerbaijan; Armenians and Azerbaijanis are massacred in interethnic conflicts

1909

The Ottoman Empire forces 60,000 Armenians into army's Labor Corps

1915

1 million Armenians living in Turkey are killed in death marches

1917

Russian Revolution; Soviet government established in Baku

1918

March: Bolshevik supporters resist nationals in Azerbaijan; thousands die

May: Azerbaijani National Council proclaims country a democratic republic; country is called Azerbaijan for the first time; Turkey begins occupation of Azerbaijan; Georgia declares independence; eastern Armenia declares its independence

September: Turkish troops march in Armenia and kill 20,000; Bolshevik supporters resist nationalists in Azerbaijan; thousands die

November: British occupy Azerbaijan

1920

Red Army occupies Armenia and Azerbaijan

1921

Red Army overruns Georgia; Stalin creates Transcaucasian Soviet Federated Socialist Republic; Abkhazia merges with Georgia

1922

USSR founded; Transcaucasian SFSR is a member; South Ossetia is designated an autonomous republic; Stalin's Great Purge of intellectuals, dissenters, and religious leaders begins

1924

Nagorno-Karabakh is created as an autonomous region within Azerbaijan

1930

Abkhazia is downgraded to the status of an autonomous republic; Soviet Union encourages Georgians to move there

1936

Transcaucasian SFSR is dissolved; Armenia, Azerbaijan, and Georgia become Soviet republics

1939–45

World War II; Stalin deports all Turks from Georgia

1953

Stalin dies

1955

Nikita Khrushchev becomes Russia's leader; allows more freedom of expression

1950s and 1960s

Oil discovered in Siberia; Azerbaijan loses role as USSR's chief oil producer; economy slows

1985

Gorbachev becomes leader of USSR, introduces glasnost; Abkhazians and Ossetians begin demonstrating for increased autonomy

1988

Armenians rally for annexation of Nagorno-Karabakh but Gorbachev refuses; Azerbaijanis massacre more than 100 Armenians in Sumgain while Armenians retaliate similarly against Azerbaijanis in Spitak; Armenian earthquake kills 35,000 people and leaves 400,000 homeless

1989

Gorbachev proposal enhances autonomy for Nagorno-Karabakh, but conflict erupts and Azerbaijan blocks Armenia's fuel supply and other imports; Georgia passes a law that Abkhazia and South Ossetia must adopt Georgian as their official languages, and students at the University of Sukhumi in Abkhazia demand that teaching be conducted in Georgian; South Ossetians demand unifications with North Ossetia while violent fighting begins in South Ossetia

1990

January: "Black January" protests in Baku by Azerbaijanis; Moscow sends troops who kill 100 Azerbaijanis; merchant ships are shelled

November: Noncommunist candidates are on the ballot in Georgia; Communist Party loses and dissident Zviad Gamsakhurdia becomes chairperson of the new legislature

December: Georgia abolishes South Ossetia's autonomous status and declares a state of emergency in Tskhinvali

The Caucasus Countries since Independence

1991

April 9: Georgia declares independence

May: Zviad Gamsakhurdia is elected president of Georgia

August 30: Azerbaijan declares independence

September 5: Soviet Union collapses; Ayaz N. Mutalibov named president of Azerbaijan

September 21: Armenians vote for independence

October: Armenia's Levon Ter-Petrossian elected president, begins to implement economic plans

October 18: Azerbaijan's Mutalibov implements declaration of independence

December: Armenians in Nagorno-Karabakh vote to create independent state; Robert Kocharian elected president of Nagorno-Karabakh; Armenian separatists declare control of the region and parts of Azerbaijan; Azerbaijan becomes founding member of Commonwealth of

Independent States; Armenians in Nagorno-Karabakh vote to create independent state; Lachin Corridor is opened

1992

January: Georgia's Gamsakhurdia declares martial law in Tbilisi

February: Azerbaijan joins with Kyrgyzstan, Tajikistan, Turkmenistan, and Uzbekistan to revive Economic Cooperation Organization

March: Khojali in Nagorno-Karabakh falls to Armenia; Azerbaijani civilians killed; Georgia's Gamsakhurdia is ousted for authoritarian leadership and flees to Chechnya

April: Abkhazi referendum calls for integration with Russian Federation; Georgian troops attack Tskhinvali, killing 1,000 Ossetians and 400 Georgians

June: All Azerbaijanis are expelled from Nagorno-Karabakh; Armenia attacks Nakhichevan enclave

June 7: Abulfaz Ali Elchibey elected president of Azerbaijan

July: Azerbaijan mounts counterattack on Nagorno-Karabakh; Georgia admitted to UN; leaders of Abkhazia declare independence; heavy fighting breaks out

September: Armenia regains land in and around Nagorno-Karabakh

October: Georgia's Shevardnadze chosen acting chairperson of State Council

1993

January: Armenian forces defeat Azerbaijani army in several confrontations in Nagorno-Karabakh; Turkey and Azerbaijan inflict trade embargo on Armenia; conflict in Nakhichevan erupts

January–March: Gamsakhurdia's followers try unsuccessfully to reinstate him by force in Georgia

February: Armenia's Ter-Petrossian dismisses prime minister for criticizing him; Hrant Bagratian named prime minister

May: Cease-fire agreement reached in Nagorno-Karabakh by Russia and the Organization for Security and Cooperation in Europe (OSCE)

June: Military rebellion against Azerbaijan's Elchivey

October: Azerbaijan's Heydar Aliyev named president; Georgia joins the Commonwealth of Independent States; Abkhazia expels Georgian militia with the help of Russia

November: Azerbaijan government introduces major economic reform program with International Monetary Fund; Georgia's Gamsakhurdia dies

1994

January: Azerbaijan concludes one-year friendship and cooperation treaty with Turkey

February: Russia granted right to maintain three military bases in Georgia

April: Agreement reached between Abkhazia and Georgia, giving Abkhazia some autonomy; 2,500 Russian peacekeeping troops move into Abkhazia

May: Azerbaijan becomes signatory of NATO's Partnership for Peace; Aliyev signs cease-fire agreement with Armenia regarding Nagorno-Karabakh

October 6: Azerbaijan's Aliyev dismisses Syrat Guseinov as prime minister; Guseinov flees to Russia; Faud Kuliyev becomes prime minister

November: Abkhazia adopts its own constitution, declaring itself an independent state

December 31: Inflation reaches 1,500 percent in Azerbaijan

1995

February: At the urging of the UN and Russia, Abkhazia announces it will not become independent of Georgia

March: Armenian government launches massive privatization drive; Azerbaijan's deputy interior minister Ravshan Javadov attempts coup, dies in process; coup fails

May: Armenia withdraws from peace talks regarding Nagorno-Karabakh

July: Armenian constitution adopted by referendum

July 19: Azerbaijan's Kuliyev resigns as prime minister; other ministers are dismissed

July 20: Artur Rasizade appointed prime minister of Azerbaijan

August: Georgia adopts new constitution that reestablishes the presidency; Shevardnadze's car is bombed on the way to sign the new constitution; he survives but the security minister is named as one of the instigators

November: Azerbaijan adopts new constitution; Shevardnadze is overwhelmingly elected president of Georgia; Abkhazia and South Ossetia do not participate in elections; Georgia imposes economic sanctions against Abkhazia

December: 30,000 Georgian refugees return to Abkhazia

1996

January: Guseinov extradited to Azerbaijan

March: Azerbaijan concludes friendship and cooperation agreements with Georgia and Turkmenistan

April: Azerbaijan joins Armenia and Georgia in signing partnership and cooperation agreement with European Union

September: Armenia's Ter-Petrossian reelected to five-year term; people protest slow vote count; Ter-Petrossian's special police kill several

November: Abkhazia and South Ossetia hold local elections; Georgia declares them invalid

November 4: Armenian prime minister resigns; Armen Sarkisian appointed as prime minister of Armenia

December: South Ossetia and Georgia agree not to use force against each other; Georgia agrees not to impose sanctions against South Ossetia

1997

January: Azerbaijan's Aliyev signs $7.5 billion contract between state oil company and a consortium of 10 foreign oil and gas reserves led by British Petroleum

January 24: Azerbaijani officials claim that Mutalibov supporters led an unsuccessful coup attempt against Aliyev in October 1996

March 6: Armenian prime minister resigns; replaced by Robert Kocharian, president of Nagorno-Karabakh

April: Fighting breaks out along border of Nagorno-Karabakh; Kocharian says Armenia might annex Nagorno-Karabakh

September: Ter-Petrossian says he is willing to compromise on Nagorno-Karabakh issue

1998

February: Armenia's Ter-Petrossian resigns in "velvet coup d'état"

March: Kocharian elected president of Armenia

October: Aliyev reelected to five-year term in Azerbaijan; Aliyev says he will settle Nagorno-Karabakh conflict based on Organization for Security and Cooperation in Europe (OSCE) proposal

November: OSCE presents new peace proposal to create a "common state" between Azerbaijan and Nagorno-Karabakh. Armenia and Nagorno-Karabakh approve; Azerbaijani officials find it unacceptable

1999

March: Azerbaijan's Guseinov sentenced to life in prison on 40 criminal counts; South Ossetia holds elections; Georgia declares the elections illegal and cuts the region's electricity supply to 30 minutes a day

October: Armenian parliament and cabinet members are killed in shooting

2000

April: Georgia's Shevardnadze reelected president

June: Iranian gunboat threatens Azerbaijani oil workers in disputed area of Caspian Sea

November: U.S. agrees to send military advisers to train Georgian military

2002

January: Russia grants citizenship to Abkhazia population and establishes visa-free travel for residents of Abkhazia and South Ossetia

April: Aliyev says Azerbaijan might consider resuming military action in Nagorno-Karabakh; Aliyev courts Russian support by offering concession on Caspian-basin natural resources

June: Iran announces decision to develop Caspian oil and gas reserves lying along the Azerbaijani shore; Russia shows support by building up military and holding war games in the area

June 18: British businessman Peter Shaw is kidnapped in Georgia as police watch

August 24: Referendum on Azerbaijan's constitution amendments provides for new secession to presidency

September: Baku-Tbilisi-Ceyhan pipeline begins construction; Russian president Vladimir Putin threatens to send military into Georgia's Pankisi Gorge region; U.S. says it will not sanction it

October 11: Georgia's Shevardnadze says he strives to restore Tbilisi's authority over both Abkhazia and South Ossetia

November: Shaw is released

December: Russia opens rail connection between Sochi and Abkhazia capital; Georgia's Shevardnadze calls it unlawful

2003

January: Shevardnadze calls for European peacekeeping troops to replace Russian troops in Abkhazia

February: Azerbaijan's Aliyev has prostate surgery in the United States; courts U.S. president's support for his reelection; International Monetary Fund and World Bank say they may cut off operations in Georgia due to corruption

March 5: Armenia's Kocharian secures reelection amid allegations of massive vote fraud

May: Armenian demonstrators support Kocharian opposition

October 15: Aliyev reelected president of Azerbaijan

November 2: Election day in Georgia. Opinion polls show that the incumbent party should lose its majority in parliament. International observers say the elections are marred by "spectacular irregularities"

November 3: Anti-government protests begin in Tbilisi demanding Shevardnadze's resignation

November 20: Government announces that two parties supporting incumbent president Eduard Shevardnadze win, affirming the majority in parliament. Protests continue.

November 23: Shevardnadze resigns. It is announced that newly elected parliament members will not be sworn in because of flawed election. Nino Burjanadze, the Speaker of the last parliament and one of the opposition leaders, is named acting president in what is called the Rose Revolution

2004

January 4: Georgia's opposition leader Mikhail Saakashvili wins presidential elections

January 14: Georgia adopts new flag

March 28: Georgia's parliament elects Saakashvili president

May 5: Ajarian leader Aslan Abashidze resigns hours after Georgian president Mikhail Saakashvili imposes direct presidential rule on Ajaria

FURTHER READING

Adalian, Rouben Paul. *Historical Dictionary of Armenia*. Lanham, Md.: Scarecrow Press, 2003, hardcover. This historical dictionary does an excellent job providing entries on persons, institutions and events, with some emphasis on recent periods, but with a view of the earliest history. There are other entries on the important aspects of the economy, society, religion, and culture. Also useful are an introduction for context and a helpful chronology.

Aghai-Diba, Bahman. *The Law and Politics of the Caspian Sea in the Twenty-First Century: The Position and Views of Russia, Kazakhstan, Azerbaijan, Turkmenistan, with Special Reference to Iran*. Bethesda, Md.: Ibex Publishing, 2003, hardcover. This book gives everyone, even those without legal or political backgrounds in this issue, an opportunity to survey the facts and history, and to analyze the legal and political realities of the present political situation of the world's largest lake.

Altstadt, Audrey L., and Wayne C. Vucinish. *The Azerbaijani Turks: Power and Identity under Russian Rule*. Stanford, Calif.: Hoover Institute Press, 1992, paperback. This book provides a unique insight into Azerbaijanis' social life, customs, politics and government.

Avakian, Arra S., and Ara John Movsesian. *Armenia: A Journey Through History*. Fresno, Calif.: The Electric Press, 1998, hardcover. This book provides a wealth of information about the Armenian people, their history, significant events, important places, and individuals who did much to make the Armenian nation what it is.

Aves, Jonathan. *Georgia: From Chaos to Stability?* London: Royal Institute of International Affairs, 1996, paperback. Investigates the power base of President Shevardnadze and the challenges he faced, including economic transformation investment prospects, ethno-regional tension, and the influence of Russia on internal affairs.

Bournoutian, George A. *A History of the Armenia People: Prehistory to 1500 AD*. London: Palgrave Macmillan, 1994, paperback. Armenia fell under foreign domination in the Middle Ages. This volume presents the differing Armenian experiences under Turkic, Persian, and Russian rule.

Braund, David. *Georgia in Antiquity: A History of Colchis and Transcaucasian Iberia, 550 BC–AD 562*. Glouchestershire, U.K.: Clarendon Press, 1994, hardcover. The first full history of ancient Georgia ever to be written outside Georgia itself, this book also serves as a valuable introduction to the substantial archaeological work that has been carried out there in recent decades.

Brook, Stephen. *Claws of the Crab: Georgia and Armenia in Crisis*. London: Pan Macmillan, 1993, hardcover. This compelling blend of exotic travelogue and astute reporting delineates peoples of the former Soviet empire struggling to transform political hothouses into cohesive nation-states.

Burney, Charles, and David M. Lang. *Phoenix: The Peoples of the Hills: Ancient Ararat and Caucasus*. London: Phoenix Press, 2001, paperback. The ancient history of eastern Turkey, Armenia, Georgia, and the Caucasus in the third and second millennia B.C. is one of the most exciting areas of archaeology today. Encounter this remarkable culture, traced in detail from its origins to its downfall. Highly illustrated, with photos and maps.

Chrysanthopoulos, Leonidas Themistocles. *Caucasus Chronicles: Nation-Building and Diplomacy in Armenia, 1993–94*. Princeton, N.J.: Gomidas Institute, 2001, hardcover. "Exile in Yerevan" is what the Greek press called the mission of Leonidas Chrysanthopoulos and his staff of three. For Chrysanthopoulos, however, his assignment as the first ambassador of Greece to newly independent Armenia was a golden opportunity to rebuild an alliance as old as history. This book is a lively account of that mission.

Coppieters, Bruno, ed. *Federal Practice: Exploring Alternatives for Georgia and Abkhazia*. Brussels: VUB University Press, 1999, hardcover. The contributors to this volume analyze the historic roots of the conflict between Georgians and Abkhazians and explore the relevance of practical federal experience from various parts of Europe in the regulation of ethnic conflicts.

Csaki, Csaba. *Georgia: Reform in the Food and Agriculture Sector*. New York: World Bank, 1996, paperback. Discusses the evolution in agricultural production in Georgia after the breakup of the Soviet collective systems.

De Waal, Thomas. *Black Garden: Armenia and Azerbaijan Through Peace and War*. New York: New York University Press, 2003, hardcover. This book objectively analyzes and chronicles events before, during, and after the war between Armenia and the Armenians of Nagorno-Karabakh on one side, and Azerbaijan on the other. The conflict was the most severe eruption of ethnic violence during the last days of the Soviet Union.

Dhilawala, Sakina. *Armenia*. Salt Lake City, Utah: Benchmark Books, 1997, hardcover. An excellent illustrated reference to Armenia, with chapter topics including: Geography, History, Government, Economy, the People, Lifestyle, Religion, Language, Arts, Leisure, Festivals, and Food. Includes a map of Armenia at back of book.

Herzig, Edmund, ed. *The Armenians: A Handbook*. London: Palgrave Macmillan, 2002, hardcover. This handbook provides a ready introduction and practical guide to the Armenians. The book includes chapters written by experts in the field, covering all aspects of the people—their history, religion, politics, economy, culture, literature, and media. Includes pictures, chronologies, appendices, maps, and bibliographies.

Hewitt, George B., ed. *The Abkhazians: A Handbook*. New York: St. Martin's Press, 1999, hardcover. The Abkhazians are an ancient Caucasian people living mainly on the eastern shores of the Black Sea in the shadow of the Great Caucasus Mountains. This book provides an overview of their history, including events after the collapse of the Soviet Union, domination by the Georgian republic, and the catastrophic war of 1992–93.

Hewsen, Robert H. *Armenia: A Historical Atlas*. Chicago: University of Chicago Press, 2001, hardcover. This traces Armenia's turbulent history, from ancient times to the present day, through more than 230 full-color maps packed with information about physical geography, demography, and sociopolitical, religious, cultural, and linguistic history.

Hovannisian, Richard G. *Armenian Van/Vaspurakan*. Costa Mesa, Calif.: Mazda Publishing, 2000, paperback. This book explores the historical, political, cultural, religious, social, and economic legacy of a people rooted on the Armenian plateau for three millennia.

Japardize, Keti, et al. *Lonely Planet Georgia, Armenia, and Azerbaijan*. Oakland, Calif.: Lonely Planet, 2000, paperback. For those interested in traveling to the Caucasus, this book is a guide to the area and is filled with historical and political facts, useful pre-departure information, a handy reference of important phrases, and authoritative advice how to stay healthy and safe.

Kettaneh, Nadine, ed. *Doing Business with Azerbaijan*. London: Kogan Page, 2000, paperback. This unique and authoritative guide to identifying and developing business opportunities in Azerbaijan includes contributions from experts, government bodies, leading banks, law and accountancy firms, as well as case studies from companies already operating in the republic.

Lerner Geography Department. *Azerbaijan (Then and Now)*. Minneapolis: Lerner Publishing Group, 1993, hardcover. Discusses the topography, location, ethnic mixture, history, economic activities, and future of the former Soviet republic of Azerbaijan.

Masih, Joseph R., and Robert O. Krikorian. *Armenia: At the Crossroads*. Santa Fe, N.M.: Blue Crane Books, 1991, paperback. A discussion of modern Armenia and its unstable political position after the collapse of the Soviet Union. Focusing mostly on the period since the democratic movement of 1988, it portrays Armenia as a nation whose future could lead down any number of paths.

Menteshashvili, Avtandil. *Trouble in the Caucusus*. New York: Nova Science
 Publishers, 1995, paperback. The book traces the roots of nationalism in
 the Caucusus and the impact of the liberalization in and ultimately the
 breakup of the Soviet Union.

Nelson, Kay Shaw. *Cuisines of the Caucasus Mountains: Recipes, Drinks, and Lore
 from Armenia, Azerbaijan, Georgia, and Russia*. New York: Hippocrene
 Books, 2002, hardcover. Recipes, drinks, and lore from Armenia, Azerbaijan, Georgia, and Russia. The people of the Caucasus are noted for a creative and masterful cuisine that cooks evolved over the years by using
 fragrant herbs and spices, and tart flavors such as lemons and sour plums.

Redgate, A. E., and Elizabeth Redgate. *The Armenians*. Oxford: Blackwell
 Press, 1999, hardcover. This book covers in accurate detail Armenia's
 3,000-year-old history with intelligence, balance, and sensitivity.

Roberts, Elizabeth, and Sharon Akiner. *Georgia, Armenia, and Azerbaijan*.
 Brookfield, Conn.: Millbrook Press, 1992, hardcover. This book contains
 double-page spreads on the states today; the ethnic and religious makeup of
 their respective populations; their history; and their current social, economic, and political outlooks.

Streissguth, Thomas, and Richard Giragosian. *The Transcaucasus*. Farmington
 Hills, Mich.: Lucent Books, 2001, hardcover. The geography and history of
 Armenia, Azerbaijan, and Georgia are presented with enough detail to give
 adequate understanding of current problems and issues that engulf the area.

Suny, Ronald Grigor. *The Making of the Georgian Nation*. Bloomington: Indiana
 University Press, 1994, paperback. The book chronicles how Georgia
 became an independent nation. This book provides an insight into Georgians, their pride in their culture and long history, and their antipathy
 toward Russia.

Swietochowski, Tadeusz. *Russia and a Divided Azerbaijan*. New York: Columbia
 University Press, 1995, cloth. Explains the long-standing Russian-Iranian
 partition of the land west of the Caspian Sea and provides a thorough cultural history of a people split by the forces of imperialism.

Thompson, Robert, translator. *Rewriting Caucasian History: The Medieval
 Armenian Adaptation of the Georgian Chronicles: The Georgian Texts and the
 Armenian Adaptation*. Oxford: Oxford University Press, 1996, hardcover.
 The first modern, annotated translation of the Christian chronicles of
 Georgia, adapted by the Armenians in the 13th century. The chronicles
 deal with the history of Georgia from its mythical origins to the time of
 their composition—and are of particular interest to the historian for the
 way they were then altered in a pro-Armenian manner.

INDEX

Page numbers followed by *m* indicate maps, those followed by *i* indicate illustrations, and those followed by *c* indicate items in the chronology.

A

Abashidze, Aslan 111, 154*c*
Abbas I (shah of Persia) 15, 145*c*
Abbasid dynasty 12, 13
Abgar (king of Armenia) 8
Abkhazia (Georgia)
  as autonomous Soviet republic 27, 31–32, 148*c*
  capital of 133–134
  civil warfare in x, 110, 133, 149*c*–154*c*
  climate of 106
  independence for 110, 151*c*
  refugees from 134, 152*c*
Abovian, Khachatur 58–59
Abuladze, Tengiz 124
agriculture
  in Armenia 27, 37, 39, 45, 49*i*, 49–50
  in Azerbaijan 30, 85–86
  in Georgia 19, 114, 115, 116–117
  pollution associated with 50, 86
Ahhiyawa people 5
Ahura Mazda (Zoroastrian god) 6, 90
Ajaria (Georgia) 111, 133
Ajarian Autonomous Soviet Socialist Republic 27
Akhvlediani, Elena 122–123
Alania 27
alcohol. *See* liquor
Alexander the Great (king of Greece) 7, 143*c*

Aliyev, Heydar 41, 77*i*, 77–79, 82, 150*c*–154*c*
Amasukheli, Elguja 123
Ambered (Armenia) 68
ancient civilizations 4–6, 143*c*
animals
  in Armenia 37
  in Azerbaijan 72
  in Georgia 106
Arabic alphabet, in Azerbaijan 30, 74
Arabic language 12, 13
Arabization 11–12
Arabs
  invasion and rule by 11–13, 144*c*
  Islam spread by 11
Aragats, Mount 35, 68
Ararat, Mount 35, 36*i*
Aras River 37–38
architecture
  under Arab rule 12
  of Armenia 54
  of Azerbaijan 91–92
  of Georgia 121*i*, 121–122
Argishti (king) 67
Armenia 35–70
  agriculture in 27, 37, 39, 45, 49*i*, 49–50
  Arab rulers in 12
  arts in 55–59
  Azerbaijan in conflict with 23, 29*i*. *See also* Nagorno-Karabakh
  Christianity in ix, 9, 52–55, 65, 144*c*
  cities of vi*m*, 39, 66–70
  climate of 35–36
  common problems in 137–141
  constitution of 42, 151*c*
  culture of 52, 55–59
  currency of (dram) 52

daily life in 59–65
earthquakes in 29, 36–37, 46, 67–70
economy of 45–52
education in 39, 50, 63–64, 64*i*
elections in 42, 43, 44–45
emigration from 46
energy resources in 46–47
environmental problems in 27, 28, 139, 139*i*
foreign aid to 48, 51, 52
foreign businesses in 50
geography of vi*m*, 35–38, 51
government of 24*i*, 42–45
health care industry in 50
independence for (1991) 42, 149*c*
industry in 27, 47, 48
languages used in 39
living conditions in 52
map of vi*m*, vii*m*
mountains of 35, 36*i*, 37
nationalism in 21
oil pipeline in 46
under Ottoman rule 20, 21, 146*c*
people of 38–39. *See also* Armenians
under Persian Empire 6–7
privatization in 48, 151*c*
regions of 36–37
revolution attempted in (1894–1897) 21
under Roman Empire 7–8
Russian relations with 44
under Russian rule 20–22, 146*c*
under Soviet rule 25, 27–29
territorial expansion of 8
in trade 47–48, 51
in Young Turk revolution (1908) 21–22